GOLF

John Jacobs driving off at Wentworth, Surrey

GOLF

by

JOHN JACOBS

(with John Stobbs)

With Foreword by

P. B. LUCAS

*Former British Walker Cup Captain
and a member of Sandy Lodge Golf Club
where the author is a club
professional.*

STANLEY PAUL
London

STANLEY PAUL & CO. LTD
178–202 Great Portland Street, London, W.1

AN IMPRINT OF THE   HUTCHINSON GROUP

London Melbourne Sydney
Auckland Bombay Toronto
Johannesburg New York

First published 1963

*This book has been phototypeset in 11pt
'Monophoto' Ehrhardt and printed by offset in
Great Britain by William Clowes and Sons,
Ltd, London and Beccles, and bound by them*

FOR MOTHER

Collaborator's Note

Working on this book with John Jacobs has been an exhilarating and rewarding experience. He first expounded his ideas in notes, articles, captions and, above all, in discussion and informal talk, much of which we tape-recorded at the time for analysis afterwards.

When he gets going about golf to a fellow-enthusiast, his real love for the game quite suddenly overflows in a torrent of vividly simple analytical phrases. We hope we've managed to catch and keep some impression of this in his book.

I'd like to thank him most sincerely for the comprehensive course on golf it all amounted to for me.

JOHN STOBBS

Contents

(Chapters 5–23 are mainly developed from articles collaborated on between us and published in the British magazine *Golfing*, of which John Stobbs was then editor, in 1958–60; so are those starred below.)

Section III   MEN IN THE FIELD

Section IV   OUTLOOK

Section V   SUMMING UP

Foreword

One evening, in the latter part of 1949, I was driving down to Chiswick in the company of the late Lord Bracken, better remembered by the students of politics as Mr. Brendan Bracken. His purpose was to persuade a thoroughly aggressive meeting in the local Town Hall that I was unquestionably the man to represent them in Parliament.

The conversation turned to our then Leader, Mr. Winston Churchill.

'I have worked with Winston in war and in peace', he said. 'What always so impresses me about him is not his oratory, or his wonderful prose, or his administrative ability but the fact that he does all three things equally well.'

And then, after a pause, he added: 'I suppose there never was such a *composite* man.'

This observation came back to me again as I was reading the script of this engaging book, having been accorded, by the author, the honour of contributing a Foreword.

The truth is that in modern professional golf, John Jacobs is a remarkably *composite* figure. He administers his expanding business from Sandy Lodge in an essentially executive way. He maintains his own game at a level which is surprising when you take account of the amount of time he is persuaded to devote to coaching. He teaches the skilled and the average, the illustrious and the humble, with a success which has earned for him, deservedly, the pseudonym 'Dr. Golf'. He expresses himself on paper or on a platform with a facility and a lack of embarrassment which places him in a category apart from all save one, I think, of his distinguished colleagues.

Here, then, is the author, but if you ever hear tell that he is really too nice a person to be a successful tournament player let me remind you of a remark he once made to my wife when he was giving her a lesson.

'It's a great pity', he said, 'that your husband ever tried to teach you to play golf. If he hadn't we shouldn't be in all this mess now.'

The searing thrust has left its scar.

As to the material in this book, I will make but three brief and disjointed comments.

First, I would commend particularly to your notice the piece about the larger, American size, golf ball. For good sense, reason and argument it would be hard to beat. Indeed, I only wish the publishers would incur the slight expense of sending a copy, with the passage suitably marked, to the Chairman of each of the golf ball manufacturing companies, and to every member of the Rules of Golf Committee at St. Andrews.

Secondly, I regard the author's picture of Henry Cotton to be not only an admirable bit of objective, incisive writing but unique in the sense that it is a generous, unbiased and quite unprejudiced appraisal of Cotton's place in the game by a member of his own profession.

Thirdly, I like this book because it uncovers for the reader those attributes of intellect and personality which have made the author not only a first-rate teacher but one of the respected 'authorities' in the professional field. A good, forward-looking mind; a preparedness to accept that there are differing ways of achieving the same result in golf and that the other man's solution may be just as sensible as his own; and an ability to introduce simplicity into complicated issues.

Moreover, throughout it all there runs an understanding, born of sharp, personal experience, of the tortures which beset the average golfer when, for the first and only time in his life, he is left with a bogey five at the eighteenth to win the monthly medal and, inevitably, takes eight.

This was an attribute, possessed to a degree by the late and beloved Fred Robson, another of the game's great teachers, whose place John Jacobs seems now so largely to have occupied.

On the eve of a Walker Cup match at St. Andrews, at the end of a day of rest and restlessness, I said to him: 'Fred, I can't stand this. You must come out and watch me hit a few before we go and change for dinner.' So off we went together, unnoticed, to a secluded part of the New Course only to find that we had between us but one peg tee, and a chipped and broken one at that.

After a few minutes of trying to balance balls on this inadequate support, Fred looked up at me and said in his inimitable vernacular: 'Now tomorrow, Mr. Lucas, in the foursome with Mr. Crawley, you'll need a peg tee so big as will take a coconut.'

An appreciation of the mental – and physical – frailties of the pupil lies, of course, at much of the base of the successful instructor. Certainly you will find evidence of it in the pages which follow; and as you read on you may also form the impression that for one who has not yet reached the age of forty, John Jacobs has amassed a knowledge of the dynamics of the swing which is unusual when you remember that the prime concern for much of his life must have been for his own individual game.

I have a feeling that this substantial treatise is only the forerunner of what may flow from this fertile mind. If such is the case, it makes an agreeable hors-d'œuvres with which to stimulate the appetite.

Of one thing I feel pretty sure. However many works may subsequently come from this refreshingly personal pen, the author will not have cause, two decades hence, to be embarrassed by the principles which now he lays before us. Not for him, I think, to cry with the Poet:

'. . . . that we but teach
Bloody instructions which, being taught, return
To plague the inventor. . . .'

London, W.1.   *P. B. Lucas.*

10

Preface

Whilst this book has never been ghosted, I believe it would never have been written but for the unfailing help and enthusiasm of John Stobbs, who twisted my arm until we got together to assemble on paper some of the thoughts and convictions I have long imparted to my pupils but rarely to a wider field. If it affords you any benefit or pleasure I assure you it is to him that we owe our thanks.

THE PHOTOGRAPHS IN THIS BOOK

Nearly all the demonstration photographs of myself, including all those in Section I, were taken specially for this book by John Stobbs.

Most of the action photographs of other players are from the files of H. W. Neale, and were originally taken by him during tournaments. 'Bert' Neale is in a class of his own in golf news photography in the British Isles. Through a decade, leading professionals and amateurs alike have become so accustomed to his presence (maroon beret, camera–case and all) and to his respect for the game and for their problems of concentration in it, that they allow him unusual licence in positioning himself to catch them playing an awkward or critical shot.

In 1962 they paid him the compliment of making him official photographer to the P.G.A. I'd like to thank him for the use of his photographs.

JOHN JACOBS

ON READING GOLF

ONE reason, I have always thought, why golf can become such a difficult game is simply because there are so many different ways of playing it *correctly*; and that one secret, for any golfer striving to improve, is to decide first which is his or her own correct way.

It is my sincere hope that this book will help any reader to do just that.

The correct way, I'm firmly convinced, is invariably the simplest. What may prove simple to one, though, may not necessarily seem simple to another.

'One man's meat is another man's poison', in fact. One of the difficulties in studying golf in books lies in learning to select from other people's experience, ideas and theories, and adapt them to your own personal needs.

I have always been an avid reader of golf books. People, luckily, have always been quick to supply me with personal bibles on the subject – a golf book being something one always itches to lend.

When I was professional to the Gezira Sporting Club, Cairo, the late Prince Jemel el Din showed me his renowned golf library. I found hundreds of 'unknowns' on his shelves; but I remember that he felt somewhat cheated that so many of his 'discoveries' should be old friends of mine!

Many books I have read have at times helped me; many more have helped me to help others. Almost all these books are similar in pattern, yet often they seem hugely contradictory.

I think I have found truth in almost every book or article I have read on golf! Yet, in spite of that fact, there is so often one thing or another in any particular book which – read by the wrong person – could bring a real setback in his or her game.

As an illustration of this, I remember two ladies, not members of my club and both strangers to me, but both good performers around 8 handicap, who arrived for tuition together. They were obviously friends, well accustomed to playing together.

I asked Lady No. 1 to hit me a few shots with a No. 5 iron; she proceeded to put the ball approximately opposite her right foot, to swing the club rather flat round her right side, to come through from the inside and make a very nice group of shots – all of which had hooked some 7 or 8 yards in flight.

When I studied Lady No. 2 in action, nothing could have looked more different. The ball was played from opposite her left foot, her swing was upright and slightly out-to-in, and her also good (though shorter) group of shots were all sliced a little in flight.

Here were two ladies with faults that I must tell each other to copy! I wanted each to try to do precisely what was wrong in the other! In other words, my instruction was of a completely contradictory nature!

Both of them, however, had repeating swings. This was why they were good players; and I wanted to interfere with this repetitive aspect as little as possible.

It had to go further than that, though. Needing contrasting advice, it followed that, since they were both avid readers on golf, they also needed different advice on what to read. I told Lady No. 1, with her too-flat swing, to read Byron Nelson's book; and Lady No. 2, with her too-upright swing, to read Ben Hogan's!

The point I am really trying to make is that it is as well to appreciate what we are doing wrong before we seek remedies by reading, from no matter how impeccable a source. Let any reader really keen to improve first see a competent instructor. When he sees you hit some shots, he will then diagnose your swing *individually*. This diagnosis is a simple matter; and though the remedial advice may not be, at least it will be tailored exclusively for *you*.

There are, I think two distinct phases of golf instruction. They are:

1. Basic principles, on which one can be fairly hard and fast, and which should make the skeleton of any good golf swing.

2. Different methods of playing the game, about which one cannot be too dogmatic.

In the recent past the golfing public has been saturated by golf books, most of which have been very good, in many ways. I feel, however, that often the titles have been wrong. Most of them should have been called 'How I play Golf'. How the writer of each book plays golf may not be the easiest way to each of his readers.

I sincerely hope that this book will make it easier for you to decide which is your own best way of playing. It is written with this in mind.

There's one more thing I want to say about it. I know people are rather used to instructional chapters in books being the simplest and most straightforward possible. But I have gone some way beyond that. In fact I have gone about as deep, in parts, as I know how to. This is because I do think that many people, including we professionals, tend to underestimate the appetite of the average golfer for real understanding of the game, as well as his willingness to apply his mind to it.

So, about the instructional part of this book, I'd like to make exactly the same point I make about lessons. In lessons I hope to teach people not just to hit the ball better, but to understand *why* they're hitting it better. I expect people to concentrate when I'm trying to help them in this way; and I ask the reader to concentrate in just the same way in order to get the best out of this book.

I hope you will find it worth while.

Setting Up Your Stance

Most golfers ruin many of their shots before they even begin to swing, simply because they set themselves to the task in the wrong way.

It really is absurd for an intelligent person to make no effort to get things right from the start. Yet most golfers don't; and here is one simple way in which they could get a much better grip on the game.

The set-up of a good shot can be learnt consciously, and without any great mental or physical effort. With a little care and application, *any one of us can set up a good swing.* Make the effort – and a good swing becomes a probability rather than an impossibility.

To begin with, grip and stance are not just 'the old, old story'. They are vital to enjoying the game – whatever level you are aiming at. Setting off to drive a golf ball with a wrong grip or stance is like trying to drive a car with the brakes on and the choke out all the time. It can be done, after a fashion, but it puts a quite unnecessary strain on the engine (which, in the case of golf, consists of the player's own muscles).

That really is what it amounts to – and it isn't really so difficult to let the brake off and unchoke the engine, once you know how to do it! Even then, to drive with one very soft tyre can make the steering pull consistently in one direction. Luckily that's easily remedied, too.

Often the lesson needed is an extremely simple one. I find again and again that when some *good* player comes to me for help, because he has been playing below his own standard, what has happened is that he has slipped out of his normally correct set up. This immediately leads him to go in for (often unconscious) counteractions.

For instance, if he slips into the habit of

Though the feet may be square, slightly closed or slightly open for a straight shot, the shoulders must always be aimed parallel to a line through the club-face to the target. The picture on the left shows this and the picture on the right shows how the shoulders swing back to their aiming position, coming into impact

aiming left, he often begins also to block the hand action, so that the ball still somehow goes fairly straight; or if he has been aiming to the right, he may have begun also to roll his wrists or shoulders in an attempt to get the ball towards the normal line.

Incorrect grip or stance, in fact, will nearly always cause some counteracting complication: and make the game doubly difficult.

Luckily, getting them right is easy. Take them in turn and there's really no reason whatsoever why all of us shouldn't get the basics right all the time.

(a) Stance Essentials

1. The first thing is to aim the club-blade squarely to the target.
2. Then lines straight through the shoulders and feet should aim approximately *parallel*, across country, to the line through the club-face to the target.
3. The shoulders must also be tilted: that is, the left shoulder must be higher than the right.
4. You should never be tense. Your stance

should, though, be firm: there should be a feeling of power, almost of the feet trying to grip the ground.
5. The stance is wider for the longer shots than the short shots: approximately shoulder-width for the woods, and progressively narrower down to approximately 12 in. for a 9-iron.
6. The way many people take up their stance they might just as well be sitting in a chair, for all the help they get from their feet and legs. The right stance gives one more of a feeling of resting on a tall shooting stick, with the back still fairly straight, and the leg muscles ready for action.

These pictures show that it is possible to aim your shoulders left with a closed stance, or aim them right with an open stance. This looks absurd as I have posed it, but many weekend golfers cannot understand why they come from out to in and slice the ball although they have closed their stance, or why they hook with an open stance. However the feet are placed, the aim of the shoulders can over-ride that, and dictate the direction of swing. On the left, the leftward aim of the shoulders is coupled with, and often caused by, having the ball too far forward. Below, the aim to the right with the shoulders is coupled with placing the ball too far back

(b) *Aim and the Shoulders*

To me, standing 'open' (body set to make it easier to hit to the left of the target) or 'shut' (to the right of the target) means much more whether the *shoulders* are open or shut, than whether the *feet* are.

If the ball is in the wrong position, the shoulders are likely to be wrongly aligned, whether the feet are right or not. If you get into the habit of putting the ball too far forward (i.e. level with or beyond your left foot for a drive) then the shoulders will turn round 'open' to face it. If the ball is too far back (towards your right foot) then your shoulders will react by swinging round into the 'shut' position. In either case, you will then be almost forced to make compensations, thus complicating your swing.

This is why it is so essential that the very first action taken at address is to aim the club-head accurately at the hole: so that you can then adjust your stance to match your aim. If you take up your stance first and only then put the club to the ball, errors creep in very easily: particularly in the relationship between your stance and the position of the ball, in relation to the correct line of aim.

If the ball is actually too far back, drawing the shoulders to the right, you will usually then aim to the right with the club as well. Contrarily, a ball too far forward makes you aim to the left.

There, quite simply, you have one cause of hundreds of thousands of hooks and slices every weekend!

Basic involuntary hooker's position: ball back, shoulders closed, blade aiming right.

These pictures are not exactly as the eye would see them. The top two were taken over my left shoulder, so the hands look further to the right than they normally are. The third was taken over my right shoulder and the hands appear further left. The top picture shows the correct lie and set of the club-face for a 5-iron aimed at the hole. The middle picture shows how, if the player places the ball a little further forward, he is apt to close the club-face and aim it left. The bottom picture shows how, if he gets the ball too far back, he can easily aim to the right

Basic involuntary slicer's position: ball forward, shoulders open, blade aiming to the left.

Note the cause here of much baffled infuriation: the man who aligns himself to the left of target will then tend to swing across the ball – and slice it to the *right*! He may then try to correct this by consciously aiming further *left*: this will probably make him swing even more wildly across it and the ball will slice all the more! The converse can just as easily happen to the man who aligns himself to the *right* of target.

(c) Summing up

At the address the blade should face the line to the target exactly. The shoulders should be parallel to this line, with the left shoulder higher than the right.

Too simple? Well, may I suggest you take a close look at the address position of the next three weekend golfers you play with. If more than one of them has just these three points of aim correct, then you are obviously playing in very good company!

I'm not saying that the right stance will guarantee a good shot. It won't, of course. But it will make it a great deal easier, just as a wrong stance will make it a great deal more difficult.

After all, it is the stance which aims the swing.

The Grip Takes Care of the Club-Blade

THE first thing to understand is that there is no such thing as one single grip, correct for everybody. Men and women with many different grips have all played winning golf.

What I (or any other professional) try to do is to put a man or woman on to the easiest grip to use with his or her natural swing-tendencies.

Now: to define the essentials. I prefer not to be at all dogmatic here. Any grip which provides for the player to connect with the ball with the blade square to the target at impact, while simultaneously allowing for full use of the hands and arms, is correct.

I set out to check any individual player like this. I always stand behind him or her (i.e. in a line with both ball and target) so that I can

see both the alignment of his stance and the direction of his swing, and can also observe the flight of the ball. From this alone, I can tell the blade position *at impact*.

If the shots are curving in their flight, even when the stance and swing are right, then the trouble is usually in the grip.

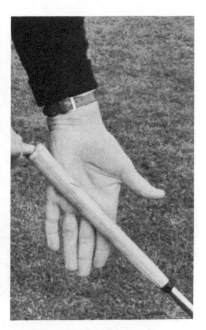

Let's take a look at the grip. It looks solid and powerful, with the hands united firmly on the shaft for sustained and reliable hitting. The first two pictures show how to take up the grip, and this is illustrated more closely in the rest of the sequence. Back of left hand to the hole. Shaft lies across the base of the first finger and runs up across the palm to pad of hand. Note: It does not run across to the base of the little finger as well, but at a higher angle, more into the fleshy part of the palm. The right hand, palm facing the hole, grips the shaft more across the top joints of the fingers than up into the palm. You can see this clearly in the arching of my right wrist in the last picture

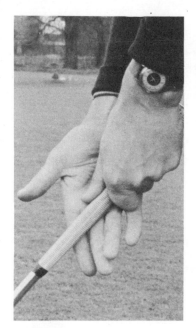
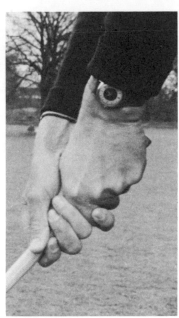
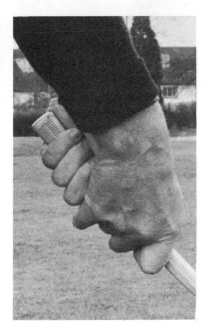

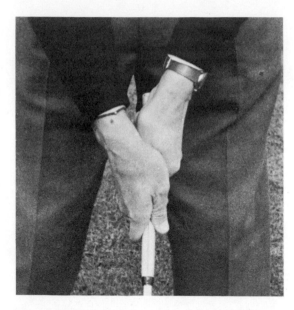

Generalising (and taking no account of special cases), if the ball is curving in its flight through the air towards the left, then the hands are likely to be turned too far over to the right (so that at address the player can see more of the back of his left hand, and of the tips of the fingers of his right than is good for him); and the correction needed is to move the Vs between thumbs and forefingers inwards past his right shoulder: even, in some cases, until they both point towards his chin, but usually not as far as that.

The converse goes for a man whose shots are curving to the right.

Anywhere between chin and right shoulder can be correct for the Vs, if it works for the player. Experiment helps to find out precisely what is best in every individual case.

The position of the Vs between thumb and forefinger in both hands should coincide. Quite a lot of variation is permissible – indeed often essential – for different individuals. The picture above shows both Vs pointing to the chin. This normally leads to a straight left wrist at the top of the swing, as below

Grip and Hand Action

How a player's wrists naturally tend to work will depend, again, upon the individual. He may naturally tend to cock them a lot on the backswing and 'throw' them on the stroke: or he may tend to keep them stiffer and straighter, and push more in the stroke with his forearms. For any player, his wrist action in the golf stroke will also depend to some

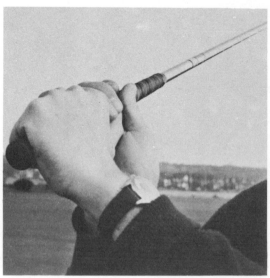

degree upon the grip he uses (which may be a wrong one for him); and, in that it is so natural and individualistic a thing, the wrist action can often only be changed to a small degree, and that by changing the grip.

The test is this: a correct grip for any player should *automatically* and naturally give him a square blade (i.e. one square to the target) at impact. Should the grip not be doing that, it will lead the player into all manner of delicate compensations.

Worse, it will make him think about them, when he should be concentrating only on hitting the ball.

He should not be worrying about trying to get the club-face back square if he feels it is open, or holding it square if he feels it is going to shut. All that sort of thing makes the game unnecessarily difficult, and probably infuriating. Even just a few open- or closed-blade shots early in a round can cause all sorts of other mistakes, through the player desperately trying to compensate for the errors he has felt already.

A correct grip can, of course, go wrong at the top of the backswing, especially if the player lets the club come loose in the fingers or between the hands when the maximum tension is pulling against them. My own

The picture below left shows both Vs pointing to the right shoulder. This is likely to lead to a cocked and arched left wrist at the top of the swing (below and above). I go into the different effects of the grips on this and the opposite page in a later chapter

advice to anyone suffering from this weakness is *not* to try to overcome it by gripping harder and harder. This often just freezes the hands and wrists completely. Instead, try to maintain the same pressure throughout by keeping the hands really close together. It is this 'togetherness' which resists 'letting go' in a good player.

Summing Up

1. The aimed club-face, and the shoulder position corresponding with it, sets the stance.
2. The stance aims the swing.
3. The grip keeps the blade square at impact.

Winding Up for the Stroke

WHAT do we want from the backswing? Simply this: that at the top of it the body, arms and hands are in a position to swing the club into the back of the ball.

The right wind-up makes it easy for the arms to hit straight through in the right plane of swing.

That is absolutely all we are aiming at.

Let's now look at what is involved – and where so many golfers make things difficult for themselves.

(i) *The First Movement of the Swing*

Leaving aside for the moment the waggle or waggles – the little dummy movements of swing in miniature which help any player to get himself relaxed and ready for the stroke – the first movement of the easy golf swing is the thing called the *Forward Press*.

It is, I want to emphasise, an integral part of *Swinging*.

It is bound up with the mechanics of the easiest way of beginning any movement. Most readers will know of the old trick whereby when you have a heavy weight to lift, if you begin by first pressing hard down on it, and then lift straight up, out of the 'press', the load seems to come up more easily.

This is nothing to do with the effect upon the weight itself. It is everything to do with the effect of the 'press' on your own muscles. It is like the similar technique we all use to move a stationary car by hand, when we first ease it imperceptibly back, the better to start it forwards.

The Forward Press is, in fact, a slight easing of body and hands into the forward swing direction, the better to recoil into the beginning of the reverse wind-up in the backswing.

It is also, and not entirely incidentally, a small reminder, or rehearsal-note, for the foreswing itself, which is going to develop in turn out of the backswing. Its general job, in fact, is to help the whole swing on the way.

Nearly every player has a forward press of some sort or another, whether he knows it or not, since it is extremely difficult to begin the backswing from nothing. But it remains a difficult thing to teach, in that it is so personal to each player.

In most cases it means turning the body slightly to the left (the follow-through side) so

Every player is going to take the club back from the ball in the way most natural for him. But there are rules to follow and the resulting swing depends greatly on the take-away. Here I am rolling back the club-head first, leading with it into the backswing and the club-face is automatically opened by the time it is half-way up

In this picture I am going back hands first – in the position weekend golfers can get into through mistakenly trying to take the club away square to the hole. The club-face is held more closed than it should be. The full effect of both methods can be seen over the page

as to get a running start at the backswing. What I want to stress here is that it is worth paying some attention to, if only to make sure that the movement into the backswing is continuous.

The backswing actually starts with the forward press; after which this little swing forward of the body, arms and hands (though not the club-head), reverses in steady rhythm into the swing itself.

Above I have started the take-away with the club-head first and then, with too much horizontal turn of the shoulders and too little tilt, reached a position of extreme flatness at the top of the backswing. Below I am showing the opposite fault. Back goes the take-away, hands first, with club-head held unnaturally towards the hole, too much vertical tilt of the shoulders and not enough turn ; and up I go into the classic floating-right-elbow position you often see lady golfers get into. On the opposite page is a correct take-away and top of the backswing position

(ii) *Winding up – in Plane*

I think the backswing is best described, and thought of, as a *swinging wrist-cock*.

You don't lift up the club; your body and shoulders wind up, quite naturally and smoothly, as you swing the club back and round and up until the limit of shoulder-turn is reached, and the momentum of the club-head pulls your wrists into their full-cocked hitting position.

Golf is a game of controlled tension, not sloppy relaxation. If the backswing is right, we shall feel tightly wound, like strong elastic, and therefore ready to deliver the blow at the ball.

A feeling of winding up the spine and muscles, while hanging on to the ground with the feet and legs, is what we are looking for. The left heel may be dragged off the ground at the top of the backswing; *but as the shoulders wind up until the back is facing the target – the legs should be resisting this turn.*

There must be *resistance* in the backswing; something for it to wind-up against, and which is ready to start unwinding it again as soon as you give the word.

The better the wind-up, the less we have to worry about that old object of attention, the left arm. Golf is very largely centrifugal, and therefore if we really wind up properly, the left arm will stay reasonably straight; it should not be rigidly stiffened anyway.

After the last chapter, I shall assume that grip and stance are reasonably sound. That being so, whether one arrives at the top of the backswing with a straight (but not necessarily flat) left wrist, or with one which is cocked under the shaft, is not important. You can be a thoroughly good player from either of these positions at the top.

Now: how about all the old problems of hip-turn, pivot, shoulder-turn, and the relationship of hands and club-head to the rest of the backswing, about which so many week-end golfers get themselves really bothered and worried? Luckily, there is a general guiding

One of the commonest faults in golf is swinging across the line to the hole from one side or the other and across the proper plane. In this sequence of pictures the shoulders are aimed left of the line to the hole. The swing follows them in a plane aimed where the shoulders were pointing. If the club-face is aligned at impact to this direction of swing the result is a pull to the left. If the club-face is square to the hole the result, as it is drawn across the ball from out to in, is a curving slice

solution to all of them, and I am going to suggest it now; it is the *plane* of the swing.

It is not in the least difficult to discover your own plane, and work on it. When you are addressing the ball correctly, the plane of your swing for that shot is that set by an imaginary straight line coming up from the ball, resting on top of your shoulders and continuing beyond them. The easiest way to see this is to look in a mirror. Stand as if you were driving directly away from it, then practise swinging back the club in such a way that as you look at it in the mirror the club-

head never leaves that ball–shoulders line, and ends in a position still in line with it above the shoulders.

If you can get this idea of the plane of the swing, then it is very easy to get the correct shoulder pivot, the right amount of hip-turn, and – very important – the correct relationship between the hands and the club-head.

For a simple example, see how if you drag the club-head straight back from the ball along the floor, with the hands leading too much, it at once goes *outside* the plane-line; while if you roll it back with a turn of the forearms, so that the club-head leads too much, it at once goes *inside* it. It should do neither of these things; it should swing back in line (or, more correctly, 'in plane') with the plane-line at every point.

Let's look closely at where this gets us.

First: at the top of the full backswing, the club-shaft should be pointing at the target (approximately – individuals must vary slightly), with both hands and club in plane. This is just how you want them, so that as you begin to unwind again into the down-swing, the hands start off swinging the club back in the right direction back down through the swing-plane to hit the ball.

Second: taking the swing of the club back to this point automatically ensures just about the right amount of pivot and wrist action, pulling against the anchor of the legs and feet.

Third: the winding-up movement can take the club-head most easily up in plane all the time, if the head and spine are kept still. They must be, and the swing must be wound-up *around* them, with no lifting or swaying – in fact in the simplest movement possible.

Fourth: you can see at once that as far as the pivot is concerned (that is, the winding around of the body and shoulders until the back of the shoulders face the hole while the club-head above them points in precisely

These pictures show what happens if the shoulders are aimed to the right of the hole. Again the swing follows them in a plane to the right of the target. If the club-face is aligned at impact to this plane the result is a straight push. If the club-face is square to the hole the result, as it is thrust across the ball from in to out, is a curving hook. This stresses my point that the aim of the shoulders is more important than the aim of the feet, for it is the shoulders which set the plane of the swing

the same direction) there is bound to be a shoulder movement intermediate between tilting them and merely turning them.

In other words, there is bound to be some shoulder-tilt, and some shoulder-turn.

These two must be balanced in the right combination if the backswing is to go back 'in plane'; and it is when they get out of balance with each other, as they very easily and very often do with very many players, that the swing leaves its own plane and the correct relationship between hands and club-head is lost.

(iii) *How Things go Wrong*

Let's take a look at how things do go wrong. This is really common sense; but observation in the mirror will help to make it even clearer. If the shoulders 'tilt' too much, that is if they turn in too much of a vertical plane, then the whole swing will be lifted above the ball-to-shoulder line, and what we call a 'too-upright' swing will result.

If, on the other hand, the shoulders 'turn' too much, that is revolve in too much of a horizontal plane, then the swing will be pulled down under the ball-to-shoulder line, and will be 'flat'.

Too much tilt: swing too upright. Too much turn: swing too flat.

Now this is important, and I think helpful; because any variation here, on either side of what I call the normal ball-to-shoulder swing-plane, has marked effects upon the ensuing relationship between club-head, arms and body.

In the too-upright swing (too much tilt, too little turn) the hands usually lead the club-head back above (or outside) the normal swing-plane-line, and the right elbow flies out like a chicken's wing at the top of the backswing. The result is loss of control and an action too steep to get into the back of the ball easily – as the club swings too sharply up and down. People who do this very often have a tendency to hit the ground, to top, pull or slice. (Yes, all these things!)

Conversely, the flat swing (too little tilt, too much turn) is usually combined with an early roll-over of the wrists, so that the club-head leads the backswing *under* (or inside) the ball-to-shoulder swing-plane. People who do this often arrive at the top of the backswing with the right elbow almost *locked* to the right side under the shoulder, so that they tend to throw that right arm and shoulder outside at the beginning of the downswing, thus causing topping, hooking, pushing, fluffing and socketing!

It really is much easier to play the game with a backswing kept, as closely as is com-

The backswing with a driver need go no further back than this horizontal position. If you think and feel that you are going just as far back as I am here, the chances are that you are actually going a bit further, since the club-head's momentum often carries it a bit beyond the point where the hands stop

fortable for you, to that ball-to-shoulder plane.

The best backswings *are*, in practice, 'in plane'; and, I repeat, they automatically set up the correct relationship between the hands and the club-head.

They also help tremendously to keep the club-face 'square' to the target throughout the swing – which is the easiest way of hitting the ball straight. 'Square' merely means in the same relationship to the hands and arms as it was at the address position, when you carefully aimed it at the target.

This I'll have more to say about later. But note here that both variations from the ball-to-shoulder plane have a complicating effect upon the aiming of the club-face at impact. The upright swing will make the blade 'shut' (that is, to the left of its correct position) on the way back from the ball and then cross

over on the way up and lie 'open' (the reverse twist) at the top. The flat swing will tend to 'open' the blade at first, but will cross it over on the way up to make it 'shut' at the top.

You can check which you are doing yourself in the mirror. If the blade or face has stayed 'square', it will be lying, at the top of the backswing, approximately in line with and parallel to the ball-to-shoulder plane line. If the toe of the club-head points across towards the horizon, though, then the blade is shut; and if the toe points downwards towards the ground, then it is open.

From either of these latter positions you can hit the ball straight. I think, though, that – especially if either comes from a too-upright or too-flat backswing – they make golf a little more difficult.

But there can be no rules exact for every player.

(iv) *How far, How fast, Where?*

What more remains to the simple factors governing the easiest and most reliable backswing?

There's WEIGHT, of course. Golfers used once to be taught to transfer their weight consciously on to the right foot during the backswing – a sort of slight sway sideways from the ball. I'm against this. I think there had far better be no *conscious* transfer of weight at all, but what you should concentrate on is keeping to that feeling you should have at the address of resting on a tall shooting stick. You should still be thus slightly 'sitting down' at the top of the backswing, with the shoulders and hands completely wound up. You should certainly never thrust your weight back on to a rigid straight right leg (nor, for that matter, forward on to the left).

What about SPEED? That's another old arguing point. So often one hears 'Slow back!' But one can go back too slowly, with the club not actually being *swung* back at all. I sometimes feel that the so-called 'one-piece method' has been taken too far and has

Remember, in a normal iron shot you are not trying for length. There is no need then for a maximum swing, but there is every need for a consistent and repeating one. If you take the right club for the distance there is no point in hitting it extraordinarily well and ending through the green. From behind the shot you can see the tighter control here compared with the driver swing. With the iron we are pinpointing the shot, not merely driving it along to a large area on the fairway

caused artificial slowness on the backswing. We all have our own speeds, in actual fact. I couldn't swing at the speed of Charlie Ward, and I don't suppose he could swing at my more leisurely pace. But in both our cases, our body, hand and arm actions are synchronised into a rhythm which suits us individually – for size, for temperament, and for the way we are put together.

A player must find his or her own speed – so long as it is rhythmic, and – I repeat – leads to a swinging wrist-cock which winds up the body, hands and arms together.

Much the same goes for the LENGTH of the swing. We all have our different length of swing, due to varying flexibility of body and wrists, and the way we let our wrists cock naturally at the end of the backswing. The best measure of what is right for any one of us is this: that our proper length of swing is the one we naturally get back to with the shoulders fully-turned, the head still, *both* hands still firmly in control of the club, the left arm reasonably straight, and the left heel not pulled too high off the ground. I am of the opinion that most people's swings are too long simply because one or more of these points is at fault.

All this amounts to the fact that the swing must be properly full, but never to the point where the lower part of the body 'gives in' during the backswing, and lets go of the sure grip of leg and foot upon the ground.

What makes a backswing *too short*, on the other hand, is any failure to reach a full shoulder-turn. The full shoulder-turn is essential to aim the whole swing at the target, and lack of it will almost always throw us outside the proper arc, to come out-to-in at the ball and much too easily pull it straight to the left, or slice it curving to the right.

(v) *Words always in Season*

When I am teaching, I continually find myself using some phrases over and over again to player after player. Since these would seem to be the ones I have found most helpful to the most players, it may be worth repeating them yet once more. They are:

1. 'Don't lift up: wind up.'

2. 'Start the backswing with the right shoulder getting out of the way.'
3. 'Point the club-head at the target in the backswing.' (This, incidentally, is a quick way of getting a beginner to pivot, and to cock the wrists.)
4. 'As near as possible, keep your feet flat on the ground.'
5. 'Stay "sat down" as you turn your shoulders.'

One last thought, which may ring a bell with one or two readers. I think golf is very akin to baseball – in this way: in baseball a player swings in plane with the flight of the ball as it comes towards him. In golf, all we have to do is to swing in plane with however far away we are from the ball – which partly depends on what club we are using. For any shot and any club, the plane most likely to be easiest really is that ranging straight up from the ball just over the shoulders, as you stand to address it for the shot.

_____

On the following pages you can see the complete golf swing in sequence from different angles. These are the points to note. In the address position the hands are opposite the ball, which is in line with the left heel. The right shoulder is lower than the left, knees flexed and the whole body in a position as if resting on a tall shooting stick. There is a general effect of firmness and readiness. In the backswing I am winding up the shoulders and the wrists. In the through swing I am unwinding the hips and wrists. In the backswing the legs have resisted the shoulder turn so as to be ready to go into action in the down and through swing. Getting the left hip out of the way allows the shoulder (still aiming straight on target), arms and hands to bring the club straight through, with the right shoulder going underneath the chin and round. The hands lead the club-head through the ball and up into the follow through. The back of the left hand is still facing the hole just after impact

33

Momentum into the Shot

Unwinding the power generated in the backswing – and swinging it into the ball.

UP to this point, I've been talking about how to address yourself to the ball for a shot, and how to swing back into a position from which you can most easily send it on its way. I described the backswing both as a 'wind-up' and as a 'swinging wrist-cock'; both of them within your own plane of swing – which extends from the ball straight up over your shoulders as you stand at the address.

Now, how to let both the wind-up and the swinging wrist-cock reverse themselves naturally into an effective golf stroke?

What is wanted *is* a reversal of what you did on the backswing. But it is not a simple one. Two things are different.

One is that although you want to unwind, and swing, back into the correct position you took up at the address, you are not going to slow down and stop there. On the contrary, your swing is going to generate an increasing momentum, all the way down until your club-head reaches its maximum speed (for that particular stroke) as it brings the club-face into the ball and on through the position where it lay.

The second is that the order of the unwinding movement of different parts of your body is not the exact reversal of their order in the wind-up.

For instance, the last thing that happened on the backswing was the completion of that swinging wrist-cock, with the momentum of the club pulling your wrists into the cocked position. About the worst thing to try to do is to reverse that as the first movement of the downswing. On the contrary, you want to save that unleashing of the hands for hitting the ball.

While the backswing builds up to a position of potential, where movement stops and then reverses direction, the downswing unleashes itself progressively into movement at top speed, discharging that potential into the ball.

(i) Starting Down

The correct start down begins in the lower half of the body – the legs and the hips. That is why telling people to 'stay sat down' in the backswing, and to 'get the left heel down first' in the downswing, is often good advice; doing so consolidates the anchor point of the feet, and starts the hips swinging back into and through the address position. This automatically begins to pull on the arms and hands and unwind them towards the ball.

Just as the swinging wrist-cock of the backswing *ended* with the actual cocking of the wrists, so the swinging uncock of the downswing *ends* with the uncocking of the wrists, as you unleash the power of your hands into the stroke.

(ii) Shoulders Back

The commonest bad shots are undoubtedly caused by the shoulders getting out of sequence! Although they obviously take their natural place in the general unwinding from the backswing, they do not swing past the ball ahead of the hands, as the hips do. They unwind towards the ball, but it is the hands and arms which swing and direct the club-head through the ball, in complete partnership with the hips. The hands and arms then, swing the club-head ahead of the shoulders, while *they* more slowly complete their revolution right through to the follow-through. On the follow-through, in fact, it is the momentum of the club-head, through the hands, which pulls them round to the finish.

In the top two pictures I am trying to show what happens if you hit early with the shoulders and roll them round. It results in a weak lunge at the ball, probably an over-late hit with the hands, and a slice or top as a reward. In the lower two pictures I am showing the correct position for the right shoulder as it unwinds in plane, under the chin and behind the hands

The commonest fault in golf, then, is the shoulders getting out of sequence, so that instead of reversing that swinging wrist-cock, the player begins to hit right from the top of the backswing *with his shoulders*.

Although this is one form of 'hitting early', it directly causes a hit 'too late' with the hands, simply because (in many players at any rate) hitting too early with the shoulders carries the hands through the ball before they have had time fully to unleash their uncocking action at it. The usual result is that the club-face doesn't have time to swing back square to the ball, makes contact still open, and a slice results.

This is often made worse by the fact that the man who hits early with his shoulders usually also rolls them horizontally at the same time, so that the right shoulder comes *round*, instead of *under* his chin, and so that his swing is thrown outside the proper arc on the way down, to cut across the ball from outside to in.

This takes us straight back, I think, to the easiest way of hitting the ball straight!

To hit the ball straight, all we need at impact is a square blade and a swing on line and in plane.

(iii) *Hitting Straight*

The beginner, and he who aims to improve his game, must have faith here. He must believe something quite simple: that there is no need to do any conscious squaring up of the blade in the downswing, or in the hitting area, with the hands! The hands should be left free for hitting the ball. The correct downswing action from the top, in the correct sequence, will take care of the blade of the club as it swings through the ball.

It really does all depend upon how the body is wound up and unwound. The hands and arms need to swing freely from the hub of the wind-up. Wind-up, then unwind, and swing the club-head while you are doing this by a free use of the hands and arms.

This type of action works for every club in the bag, allowing the loft on each to do the work as necessary.

(iv) *Hitting Clean*

We need to be in plane to hit the ball cleanly.

The swing must come back in the right arc to match the player's address position. He must be hitting the ball with the club-head attacking from somewhere behind the shot, as it were; but his club-head must neither be approaching it at too steep an angle, nor at an angle too close along the ground.

If the club-head comes in too steeply, he will tend either to chop down on the ball, or to hit it on its top with the club-head still on the way to the bottom of the swing. On the other hand, if the club-head comes in on an arc too flat along the ground, he will be liable to fluff the shot by hitting the ground behind the ball, or else to top the ball, this time by catching it with the bottom edge of his club already on its way up, after passing through the bottom point of its arc.

The swing mistakes which cause these more-difficult approaches to the ball are as follows: hitting too late with the wrists and hands, thus steepening the club-head's arc into a last-moment dive attack on it; and hitting too early with the wrists and hands, thus flattening the swing along the ground before it gets to the ball.

Do note this, though: the wrist action in the hitting area is very closely bound up with the general aim and action of the swing. If the stance and swing so far have been square, that is, correctly aimed at the target, then the hands can follow a normal action and hit the ball straight. But if the stance and/or swing has been aimed markedly to the right, then the hands and wrists will tend to roll in the hitting area; while if the general aim or swing has been to the left, the wrist and hand action will tend to 'block' in the hitting area.

Both these variations make golf more difficult!

(v) *Getting the Left Side out of the Way*

You may have heard quite a bit about 'hitting against the left side'. I don't say that that is never good advice. But it does depend on who you are, and how you naturally swing. For the player who opens the face of the club at the top of the backswing, the idea of hitting against the left side can help; in order to hit the ball straight, he has to roll his hands and wrists into the hitting area, and the idea of hitting against the left side will help him to do this.

For most people, though, I think it is better and more reliable advice to think of 'getting the left side out of the way', in the hitting area. If you do this, you make more room for the arms and hands to come through. Though still allowing the full application of wrist-power into the shot, getting the left side out of the way slows down any tendency to roll the wrists (right over left) as the power is applied, and thus makes it easier to swing the club-face squarely through the ball and on into the follow-through.

Most good players do clear the left side out of the way before the actual stroke, *but their shoulders still await their turn in the swing*, with the right shoulder then swinging *under* the chin and not *out and round*.

People who 'tense up' at the mere sight of a ball, again, can still often be helped by being

The top picture shows the left hip well out of the way, allowing plenty of room for the arms and club to swing through towards the target. This is the correct way to do it. The other two pictures show what happens if you try to hit against a firm left side. You can only get the club through to the target by snapping and rolling your wrists – a much more difficult way to play golf

told to hit against the left side – merely because it can be one way of stopping them from turning their shoulders right from the top of the backswing – a habit we were talking about just now.

To many people this getting the left side to swing clear, out of the way, so that hand and arm action can come through unrestricted while the right shoulder is still swinging under the chin, is the most difficult part of the game. 'Hips out of the way and right shoulder under' describes, to me, very much the feel of the down and through swing, however. This allows the whole of the right side to come into the shot, *behind* the hit, giving, incidentally, maximum power and momentum, and an easy sweep on into a full follow-through.

(vi) *From Impact to Follow-through*

In the good golf swing, there must be freedom. Not just that which comes naturally from getting the left side out of the way, so that the right side can swing through after the ball and into the full finish, but also that from a sensible use of the head.

Certainly, you want to keep your head still until the ball is struck and away; but any attempt to glue it down to the bitter end is going to restrict your action through the hitting area, and cut down the free follow-through which should follow.

The effects of that will carry right back into the actual stroke, and you will lose both power and accuracy. If the stroke is anticipating a spavined follow-through, it will also anticipate, in its own action, some of the same weakness. The golf swing and the actual stroke alike demand freedom if they are to fulfil themselves naturally and completely.

As long as the hit is under (by which I mean very much like a straight bat in cricket), the swinging of the left hip out of the way will allow for complete freedom of hitting with the right hand, without any fear of rolling the club-face.

(vii) *The Ladies Differ*

Incidentally, for ladies the downswing does tend to be slightly different. Even the best of them usually begin to uncock the wrists earlier in the downswing than men need to, in order to reach maximum speed at impact. This is simply because their wrists and hands are not so strong as men's are. Consequently, since the club-head widens its arc into the ball, due to this earlier straightening of the wrists, many of the leading ladies tend to come up on to their toes at impact, simply in order to make room for that wider club-head arc to get into the ball without hitting the ground first. By coming up on to the toes they give their club-head that much more room to swing cleanly forward into and through the ball.

(viii) *Individuals Vary*

This brings us back to one of the most important things in any attempt to help other people with their golf – including this one!

Discussing simple sound general principles is one thing: teaching and applying them to particular individuals is quite another. And because there is no one distinct way of playing and swinging, the written word can never be as effective as the lesson from a competent professional.

Any good swing must balance individual variations within itself. To take two extreme examples: swinging with a blade shut at the top of the backswing may call for coming through with hips turning more towards the hole at impact than usual; while swinging with a blade open at the top may call for much more of the feeling of hitting against a firm left side.

The good instructor will not normally – in my opinion, anyway – tamper with the things a player does naturally. For instance, it does not matter whether the wrists are under the shaft at the top of the backswing or not – so long as the blade is brought back to square in the hitting area. The whole movement of any

In medium and short iron shots the bottom of the swing should be just beyond the ball (a good player's divots always extend beyond the spot where the ball lay). I am demonstrating here the correct arc of the swing, leaving the loft of the club to give the ball elevation

individual's swing has to be balanced to give a square blade and a straight-through swing at impact – in the simplest fashion *for that person.*

That is one more reason why – again in my opinion – the keen weekend golfer should seek, and take, much more advice from his club professional than he or she usually does.

(ix) *The Usefulness of Practising*

When talking of practice, here, I am assuming that the reader plays just for pleasure, and has neither taste nor time for practising on the scale and with the determination a young professional needs to forge his game.

I personally love practising. I love experimenting, which probably helps my teach-

ing – if not my playing! I have discovered, though, that if I find myself practising badly, I must stop for a little while, and try to re-create a simple mental picture of exactly what I am trying to do.

This need for a mental picture, of course, goes right through all golf. We must have it, every time, both for the execution of each shot, and also of the flight of the ball. We must see in our mind's eye exactly what we are just about to do. This is particularly important in short shots, where we must picture both the flight and the roll required. The same goes for the putt; we must picture the line and how the rolling ball will take any borrow.

In practising your full golf swing, you want to rely, to begin with, on the mental picture

A tremendous number of otherwise competent golfers try to hit the ball up with medium and short irons, throwing the club-head through the impact area ahead of the hands as I am doing here

your instructor will have given you – of how *you* can best swing the club. Your practising to learn this swing can mainly be done with one club. A 6-iron, for instance, is fairly easy to use; but the stroke with it contains all the ingredients of a full swing. What you need is pure repetition of the mental picture given, and – so long as you do not begin to lose interest – as much of it as is needed to get the swing completely right and repetitive.

Most of the world's leading players have done this, at the stage of their 'grooving' period, even if later in their careers they reserve more of their energy for actual competition – as do nowadays Locke, Thomson and others who very rarely play more than 18 holes practice in one day. At their stage, where their swings have settled down, they need just short spells, going right through the bag of clubs one by one, to keep the rhythm and the swing ticking over.

All through your life, though, the short game – the 'feel' part of the game – needs constant attention if it is to keep up to your best standard. This is a lesson I might as well teach myself; for I find, now that I spend so much time teaching, that although my long

In the picture below I have posed the impact position of the action sequence above. It shows quite clearly that the ground is getting in the way at the bottom of the swing and the divot will begin before the ball is hit

There are times when you want the bottom of your swing directly under the ball, like this short, open-faced pitch over a bunker to stop quickly on the green

game seems to stay put, chipping and pitching quickly leave me if I don't keep practising them.

Obviously, too, time spent practising putting is time well spent. We have always been taught that the putting stroke should be a smooth one. But this is not enough in itself. The gentle stuff, with lots of follow-through, is fine if the putting surface is perfect. But with anything less than a perfect surface, the stroke must have more authority.

(x) *Keeping Golf in its Right Place*

Golf being the difficult game that it is, it is very easy for any of us to lose our sense of proportion about it. I seem to meet far too many people who regard as a disaster of the first magnitude a couple of fluffed pitches or a drive into the rough. In point of fact, of course, the greatest players hit very few shots completely as they intend to; and I think it does much for our temperament in golf if we realise and accept this. I often want to say to one of my pupils: 'Who are you to think you can do more than they can!'

If golf is a difficult game, however, we should all be the more grateful for our good shots. After all, the game is tougher than any of us – and will always win. The best players will follow a sparkling 64 with a puzzled 75; or will win a tournament one week – and fail to qualify the next!

Try hard we must – but we must also keep a sense of proportion!

In each of the pictures below and over the page I am demonstrating a definite fault. After reading the first four chapters you should be able to recognise them. Why not write down your own reactions and compare them with my own summing up overleaf?

I

2

4

3

1. Overswinging. 2. Swinging back outside the correct plane. 3. Swinging back inside the correct plane. 4. Outside the correct plane again. 5. Inside the correct plane. 6. Rolling the right shoulder up and round instead of unwinding it under the chin. 7. Legs too straight, hands too low, body bent too far over. 8. That right shoulder roll again

In these chapters some of the main points and themes which come up again and again in teaching players of all kinds are taken one by one and discussed a little more fully.

Check your Grip and Hand Action

OFTEN it would seem to me a good plan for us golfers to become introspective about our games; to stop, think, and make quite sure to ourselves that we know just what we are trying to do.

It can all seem so complicated. We have read and listened to so much advice, yet somewhere on the way most of us keep losing touch with the fundamentals.

What, after all, are these? Put very simply, I would say that with all our full shots we are aiming to swing the club-head straight through the ball on line, and to have the blade square to that line. Move a stage further: and the ability to swing the club *straight through* is largely dependent on pivot. The right sort of pivot, however, is largely dependent on the correct stance; and to be able to present the club-face squarely to the ball depends largely on the hands and wrists. This, in turn, is dependent on the right grip!

On the one hand, then, we have stance and pivot; on the other grip and wrist action. It is obvious, then, that these two factors are inter-related. But for the purposes of simplicity and clarity, I am going to split the two, discussing here only the grip.

As someone who tries to teach golf, I want to make clear at the outset that I am not in the least dogmatic about everyone gripping the club in the same manner. Indeed, anyone who was so dogmatic would be making the mistake of assuming that we one and all are blessed with the same ability to swing the club. If that were the case, all the best players would have the same grip and the same swing — which they do not!

Let's keep in our minds the two functions of a golf grip:

1. *To present the club-blade squarely to the ball.*
2. *To provide as much club-head speed as possible.*

How to do it? Many great players have overlapped the little finger of the right hand over the first finger of the left. Others, instead, interlock these same two fingers. There have been those who use a two-handed grip; and also some who use palm grips, with the thumb of the left hand round the back of the shaft. Obviously this is all a matter for personal choice.

Most good players of today use what is accepted as the Harry Vardon overlapping grip, and I would personally recommend it to any beginner, because it is the easiest grip to create the club-head speed wanted and keep

These three pictures show what can happen if you grip the club with the Vs too far to the right. Your wrists are over-cocked at the top of the backswing and there will be a definite tendency to close the club-face at impact because that is the way your hands will naturally be trying to turn

the blade square at impact. But it still may not suit *you*, and don't be afraid to experiment if your shots are weak and off line.

There is, though, one part of the grip that with all good players would seem to vary the least: namely, the angle of the hands on the shaft. This angle is shown by extending the lines, or Vs, between the thumb and fore-finger of each hand upwards, and observing to which part of the top portion of the body they point.

Here I would stress there are definite limits – towards the point of the right shoulder on the one extreme, and towards the chin on the other. Whatever grip we are using, it could be termed correct if it keeps the hands from straying outside these limits, and the desired results are being attained. Watch then that

your present grip is doing this for you and if you are not wholly satisfied, don't be afraid to experiment.

I am reminded of Carnoustie, 1953, when I saw Ben Hogan for the first time. Having avidly digested his book *Power Golf*, I was then already a confirmed disciple. But I noticed at once that he had changed his grip considerably in the period since his book had been published. After his appalling car accident, he had had to change his method slightly, and this had called for a change of grip. Both of these grips brought him great success.

We must remember that the basic idea of a golf grip is that you should hold the club at address in the same way as you intend to apply it to the ball at impact.

It follows then that if we are actively pre-senting a shut blade to the ball at impact, and our shots are accordingly *bending* to the left, then our hands must have turned more to the left at impact, than they were at address position. If this is happening to you, try then, first of all, moving the hands over the shaft to the left at address. Of course, the opposite will apply just as well, in reverse.

I say, *first of all*, and if it were as simple as that it would be very easy. But it *is* surprising in how many cases this first stage is the whole remedy. Many golfers play for years with a grip that fails to present the blade square to the line of swing, and one can appreciate that getting a reasonably straight shot in these circumstances means putting the line of swing out of true, to balance the blade position. Hence so many out-to-in open-blade players (I did stress, you'll remember, that grip and pivot were inter-related).

One more point I wish to bring out is that the type of grip we employ has a very large bearing on the type and amount of wrist action. In most cases, the further the hands (i.e. the Vs) lie to the left at the address the less wrist-cock there will be, as opposed to when they are both turned over the shaft towards the right. I have seen players get the blade of the club actually more open, both at the top of the swing and at impact, by putting the left hand a little more over towards the right at address. This gets the left thumb out of the way and allows for a cupping of the left wrist at the top of the backswing, and is just one instance where a change of grip completely changed the way the hands will be used to control and swing the club.

There are indeed many possible combinations of grip and wrist action – all correct so long as they produce a good result. The only thing really to avoid is getting the hands *too much over* or *too much on top* of the shaft.

As for wrist action, I am convinced it should be very largely passive during the golf swing – finding the grip that suits you will ensure that your hands take care of themselves. Sam Snead, when recently asked how he had played so well for so long, replied: 'Because my hand action has always been passive.' This could be an excellent rule for most of us – once we have found the most suitable grip to give us both power and a square blade at impact.

If the grip is taken with the Vs aiming to the left of the chin your hand action is limited. At the top of the swing the left thumb is right under the shaft and limits the wrist cock. From this position it takes a very strong player to get the club-face square again at impact and the average golfer will almost certainly hit the ball with the club-face open

Stance
and
Pivot

THE two main functions of a pivot seem to me to be these: firstly, that it should give the hands and arms their path back from the ball and then forward through the ball; secondly, that it should help to time the action of the hands and wrists.

In short: *the body should be wound up* FROM *the target and unwound* TOWARDS *the target.*

If this is done correctly, then a correct use of hands and wrists will be greatly encouraged. The wrists will be cocked at the top of the backswing, and will be uncocked through the ball along the line of flight. But remember: just as surely as good hand and wrist action

depend *basically* upon the right grip, the very first requisite of good body action is a good stance.

Certainly I find that by far the most faults I undertake to rectify amongst my pupils originate with the stance. So many players I find are never, to start with, in an address position which makes a wind-up *from* and *to* the target possible.

When I talk of stance I am also including correct ball positioning, and aiming. This is important because it is so common for pupils to concern themselves only with their feet when lining up – *and neglect to aim the club-blade!* Since it is the blade which will eventually hit the ball, it is imperative that this should be correctly placed – *at right angles to the intended line of flight.* With an iron club this means the bottom edge of the blade, not the top.

In these two pictures you have the key to straight driving. You must start from an address position from which it is easiest to wind up 'on target'. You can see how the stroke has swung straight through towards the distant pylon I aimed at

Harry Weetman (left) and Bernard Hunt (below) show two extremes in the length of backswing. Weetman has a free, supple swinging wrist-cock with the right elbow away from the body. Hunt has a short, tightly controlled backswing with the hands holding on very firmly to limit the cock. But both are thoroughly wound up for the stroke

Harold Henning (left), the South African professional, fully unwound towards the target at the end of a drive. Note how his left side has got right out of the way to let the right side come cleanly through

51

If the blade of the club is correctly placed, then the ball will be more likely to be in a correct position in its relation to the feet. We seem to fall into two main errors over this, and either have: (*a*) the blade aiming to the left with the ball too far forward in the stance; or (*b*) the blade aiming right with the ball too far back.

Once we fall into either category, it is pretty nigh impossible to pivot directly to and from the target – and this is what should be our aim. Looking at it more closely we shall soon see why. With the ball too far forward the shoulders will point too much to the left at address and will set in motion a steep out-to-in pivot. With the ball too far to the right at address, the result is often a too flat, too much *inside* pivot.

I think the best way to feel at address is that of playing down a railway line with the ball on one track and the shoulders parallel to the intended line of flight over the other. Try always to get this feeling of having the shoulders approximately parallel to your line of direction, each time you address the ball.

At the same time, see that the left shoulder is distinctly higher than the right. In other words – anticipate your hitting position! It sounds very easy, and quite elementary, but it does give you a sense of being the 'hub of the wheel'.

If one can grip the club correctly, and then stand and aim correctly, the overall feeling is then of winding up the top half of the body in the backswing, and unwinding the bottom half in the downswing.

I don't think I could close this short explanation better than by quoting Cary Middlecoff's *Advanced Golf*: 'The body movements on the backswing are made for the purpose of getting the hands into the proper position and working in the proper tempo. The movements of the downswing can be said to be for the purpose of getting the body out of the way so that the hands can follow the proper course.'

Wind Up — Don't Lift Up

How often do we all hit shots far below our normal standard at the most crucial point of the proceedings! It is a lack of confidence in ourselves, and I am sure it almost always results in causing players to curtail the backswing of whatever particular shot they are playing.

Yes, that quick jab is so often shortage of backswing, rather than 'head-up', as it is so often loosely described.

In my own instance I find myself frightened of a 40–50 yard pitch off a bare lie; it takes real courage to let the club swing back far enough to keep it smooth on the way through. Then I try to bring to mind a picture of Ken Bousfield playing the shot in his delightful unhurried fluent manner.

The real benefit of a complete wind-up is that it allows the player to attack the ball in

Only a complete wind-up really gives you a chance to 'attack the ball in the back', as I like to put it. Make sure you get a full shoulder pivot with hips and legs resisting. Far left: Ben Hogan. Above: Sam Snead. Left: Ed Furgol (who cannot straighten his left arm since a childhood accident). Below: Ken Bousfield winds up fully even for short pitches. Overleaf: myself

the back. After all we want the ball propelled forward, so it follows we should hit it in the back. Lack of pivot produces a swing too narrow for this, giving rise to a steep downswing, which will only hit the ball a downward glancing blow.

If the shoulders are not completely wound up we see that the club will be pointing away to the left of the desired line at the top of the backswing. It is precisely this direction that the downward chopping stroke will take, producing invariably a bad pull with a short iron and a pretty powerless slice with everything else.

A still further benefit of a *completed* backswing is the resultant feeling of being wound up, which is in itself a powerful feeling and therefore alleviates the desire to hit too hard, too early, in the downswing. One can feel there is sufficient room to apply the club to the ball without giving that sudden jerky application which is fatal.

When teaching, I get pupils to finish the backswing completely, before starting the downswing, by asking them to point the club-head consciously at the target before starting down. This virtually ensures a full shoulder pivot and a complete wrist-cock.

Indeed, I often go even further, and suggest that the club-head be pointed to the *right* of the target, to make sure that the shoulders are wound up to a maximum. That takes confidence; most players find it easy to do on the practice ground, but astonishingly difficult with a 5-iron to the last green when the game is square. Even David Thomas at the 71st hole in the 1959 Open at Lytham St. Annes, with a 7-iron to the green, was a tragic example of no wind-up at the crucial moment. The club was picked up outside and the ball hit straight left into trouble. A straight No. 7 iron shot would probably have crowned his already great performance with the 1959 Open title!

To sum up: it takes courage and confidence to wind up; but – if it is done correctly – a feeling of power allied to a feeling of compactness should result. It is this feeling of being compact but still powerful which, in the vital moment, can give the player the confidence which makes all the difference.

Wind up, don't lift up. It takes courage.

Under and
Out
of the Way

I HAVE often asked myself what is common to all good strikers of a golf ball. The only thing I can find which they all seem to do is that they hit *under*. By that, I mean that the right side relaxes and swings under a taller left side through the ball.

This means that in the hitting area the shoulders are tilted, and yet the left hip is turned to some extent towards the target so as to get the body out of the way sufficiently to allow the hands and arms room to hit through.

I would stress that this setting up of the correct body position is to give the hands and arms a chance – after all, they and they alone can apply the club-head to the ball. It is when the body, particularly the top half at the shoulders, is doing too much of the hitting that it gets out of position.

Golf, I believe, is the difficult game it is, partly because the shoulders and the hips do not work in the same plane through the ball.

Trying to swing 'under', purely and simply, so often leads to the left hip getting blocked in the hitting area, which in turn blocks the arms and causes the wrists to roll instead of to hit out to the target.

On the other hand, if too much stress is put on clearing the left side, the right side will get outside early in the downswing, again not allowing the hands and arms to hit through on line.

Let me now try to define the downswing. To allow the right side to swing under, the first thing to do in the downswing is to move the hips laterally to the left. This can only be achieved by good leg action. This is the *under* part of the swing. The start down with the

The low swing through the ball, demonstrated above by Max Faulkner and left by Bernard Hunt. The essence of this position is that the left hip rolls round while the right shoulder rolls under

Here I was trying to help the French international Mlle. Brigitte Varangot, who had been moving her head slightly forward in the downswing, which in turn was causing her to hit round, not under. I was holding the left shoulder, stopping it from going round

lower half of the body will have brought the hands and arms down to hip height, leaving the shoulders behind.

From here we concentrate on the *out of the way part* as we cut loose with the hands and arms. The head, I hardly need to say, must remain still during all of this. Indeed, if there is a secret to hitting under and past the body it is to keep the head *behind* the ball until the ball is on its way.

Don't be a Statue!

ARE we not getting far too position-conscious and forgetting the all-important thing – to swing the club?

We have had in the recent past a spate of golf books, full of positions which dissect the golf swing. These books, I feel sure, give the impression only of *position* and never of *swinging*. It is important to remember that the players shown in this way *swing through* the positions you see in the books, and I suppose never really feel the different positions you see when looking at the pictures.

Now, all too frequently these days, we see potentially great golfers putting themselves into that late hitting position of a Hogan and a Snead. This sort of thing is of no value whatsoever! In fact, I would say it is harmful, in that anyone who tries to *put* himself into this position has so obviously missed the reason why the great players are able to swing this way.

The wrists are *not* consciously held back in

the downswing until the last moment. This really is too difficult to do. Learn to swing and swing correctly, and the wrists will uncock at the right time. I get the impression that many of our young players, particularly assistants, are making a conscious effort not to let the club-head work in the hitting area. In other words they are so keen on late hitting that they are never actually using the club-head at all – despite the fact that hitting is surely the most natural thing to do with the club-head, certainly more natural than trying to hold the club-head back!

Grip, stance and pivot should allow for the hand and wrist action to be absolutely natural, not forced in any way. If you feel you have to hold the club-head back consciously, *then there is something wrong*, and you are certainly not *swinging*.

In the past we have seen many unorthodox *swingers* playing great golf. The very fact that they have been swinging has helped to keep them in the groove. I feel sure these players have never become too much bogged down by position. If you are in a wrong position, then certainly try to *swing* through a better one.

But, whatever you do, don't try to *put* yourself into a better position!

A golfer's waggle usually gives the show away, proclaiming whether he is a swinger or not. The non-swinger is so stilted that we know he is going to go from one position to the next, and never swing the club at all.

The top of the backswing and halfway-down positions seem to be the most sought after. How often do we see a player admiring that late hitting halfway-down position he has put himself into! He can feel where he *should* be. I venture to say that the finest players never feel this position; they feel a much more complete thing, that of swinging the club-head through the ball to the target. We all freely discuss our golf swings but how many of us have *swings*, or have we just a set of positions?

Now if you have decided to swing, don't get too relaxed. There has to be resistance to swing, and that is why I feel golf is a game of tension. Obviously there must not be too much tension, but not complete relaxation either. Learn to *swing firmly*, correctly, and never sloppily.

The Right Elbow

NINETY-NINE per cent of floating right elbows – the ones that stick up or out like a chicken's wing – are caused by an incorrect pivot. If you *tilt* your shoulders instead of partly *turning* them, and take your hands back ahead of the club-head, then you will get a floating right elbow.

Controlling the elbow won't necessarily put the thing right, since it is caused by a combination of pivot and of wrist action following the pivot, which leaves the club-head behind on the backswing. You can correct it by getting the club-head on its way back first, so that it leads the elbow into the right position, which then feels strong while you turn.

You could, of course, hit good golf shots with a floating right elbow, as long as the elbow gets into the right place to hit the ball. That magnificent player, James Bruen, for instance, had a champion floating right elbow, but always still managed to get it into the right position to hit the ball with. So, nowadays, to a lesser degree, does Jack Nicklaus.

But only a right relationship between hands and body can put you into the right position in the easiest way.

When teaching people, there is quite a simple general rule I follow: in both cases,

THE FLAT, TIGHT ELBOW

Rolling the club-head back first can lead you into a flat position at the top, with the right elbow tightly jammed into the side

EVERYTHING IN BALANCE FOR POWER

Here I'm showing a correct pivot and hand action, leading naturally into a correct right elbow position at the top

THE UPRIGHT, FLOATING ELBOW

A steep shoulder tilt, instead of a proper pivot, into the backswing usually leads you straight into an upright position at the top, with the right elbow floating madly

floating right elbow and too-tight elbow, I use what *sounds* like a local independent variation merely to wipe another one out, in its effect when the player tries to do it. You tend to get a floating right elbow if you leave the club-head behind your hands. If you then try to start back club-head first, you often cure it.

Other things being equal, of course, faults can come from both variations. If I drag the club-head back, that's when I float it: if I start the club-head back too much ahead, I go flat.

If you don't get the club-head moving on the way back, then you can't get back to the top of the swing without moving the right elbow out from the body; and the delayed club-head thus nearly always leads you to a steep position. You can easily spend five minutes explaining this to a player; and he can easily follow it and see how it all works.

There are actually thousands of people with this sort of trouble, because those who have read about and studied the game have been so much told to 'take the club back in one piece'. Trying to do just this, if it is misunderstood, can lead the player straight into a floating right elbow!

With this particular fault, as with so many others in golf, we come back to just one basic thing. May I repeat myself once more and say it again: The relationship between your club-head, your hands and your body is vital. *If you get the right relationship between your club-head, your hands and your body, you will never get a floating right elbow.*

That American Method

MANY readers I know will have watched the 1960 Curtis Cup at Lindrick. Many more will have seen some of the matches on television. Everyone in these islands was disappointed we lost, but surely this time we learnt a lesson. I say this because the similarity of method of the American team must surely have been obvious to everyone.

In the last decade I feel sure that this has

This picture of American Curtis Cup player Barbara McIntire illustrates very clearly what I have said in this chapter

Two more of America's Curtis Cup team pictured at Lindrick in 1960. They are Joanne Gunderson (left) and Judith Eller (below)

become true of all U.S. teams. Their best players are becoming very standardised in their methods. This was particularly true of this team in that, by their age, they had all learnt the game in the last ten years.

Now what is this method employed?

1. First, it is devoid of all frills and complications.
2. It is based on a sound grip of the club.
3. A good stance.
4. The club is taken back by the shoulder pivot and straight left arm.
5. The club is brought through by the unwind of the hips and a straight right arm to the target.

Now where does this method differ from the British concept of the golf swing?

Emphatically: in the hitting area and just afterwards. I would pick this out as the chief difference between U.S. golf and our own.

In this country we try to hit the ball with the hips square and the hands squaring up the blade at impact. In America, the grip is given the job of keeping the blade square. In the hitting area the hips are much more open to the target, to allow for the right arm to go through. Indeed the whole of the right side comes through to the target.

I want to leave it at that, so that this chapter shall be devoid of all frills and complications. But to sum up: a good grip and stance; the club is swung back by winding up the shoulders and keeping the left arm straight; it is swung through by *unwinding the hips*, which allows for a straight right arm to go through to the target.

The Odd Paradox in the Backswing

How should the club go back? I am very often asked this question; and of course, as with so many similar questions, there is no definite answer.

What I will try to do, then, is discuss backswings generally, and various types of backswings, with a particular accent on the club-face position.

Generally speaking, the *direction* along which the club goes back should be determined by the shoulder pivot. This is very close to saying that the start back should be in one piece – but it is not quite the same thing.

While the *direction* of the backswing is governed by the shoulder turn, the *width* of the backswing is partly determined by how soon and how much the wrists cock. The backswing, in fact, consists in the main of these two factors, shoulder pivot and wrist-cock. The left arm maintains the radius of the swing, while the use of the wrists controls the width of the club-head arc.

The shoulders, in pivoting through 90°, should drag the hips approximately 45° round, and may also pull the left heel off the ground as the top of the backswing is reached. All this, of course, has to be done while keeping the head still.

Now let us take the two extremes of backswing.

Usually a flat shoulder-turn is accompanied by a roll of the left forearm, and a quick opening of the club-face. In this type of

Human mechanics haven't changed. In 1900 J. H. Taylor, in his book 'Golf Faults Illustrated', used these pictures to show the difference between the flat swing (left) which opens the club-face on the way back, and the upright swing (right) which keeps it closed longer. At that time Taylor believed in the flat swing with an open stance

swing, at the halfway-up position, the club follows the flat shoulder turn, to cut more inside than normal; and the club-blade, at this stage, will be more open.

What usually happens from this position, is that the club carries on in the same plane (flat, remember) and finally arrives at the top with the club-blade in what we accept as a *shut* position, with the left wrist straight, and not under the shaft. (Like Bernard Hunt's.)

Ben Hogan's backswing is of this general type; he, however, makes it into a more upright position by cupping his left wrist

early part of the backswing, to roll the left forearm the other way, *into* the ball, thus holding the club-face more shut. At the halfway-up position, the club will be much straighter back from the ball (less 'inside' than in the flat swing), and the club-face will be more shut.

From this halfway-back position, though, the club is usually carried on in plane – upright, remember – and arrives more open at the top than it does from the ordinary flat swing.

The wrists, in this type of action, arrive

Henry Cotton. A grand swing which is a combination of two tendencies. He takes the club back well inside the line, opening the face early like a flat swinger. But he then shifts to an upright movement as he carries the club to the top, all part of his belief in lively wrist and hand action. (Pictures from 'My Swing', Henry Cotton, Country Life, 1952)

under the shaft at the top of his backswing, thus opening the club-face.

Another variation of this type of backswing is when, from the halfway-up position, the hands and arms are lifted into a more upright plane than the first half of the backswing. We then arrive at the top in a particularly open-bladed position, due to its quick opening early in the backswing. (Like Henry Cotton.)

Now for the other extreme.

An upright shoulder-turn will tend, in the

more under the shaft at the top than in the flatter swing, although not necessarily with a cupped left wrist. Byron Nelson would seem to be a first-class example of this type of backswing.

There is thus a paradox inherent in both two normal extremes of shoulder action. A flat-shoulder-pivot swing starts open-faced, ends shut; and upright-shoulder-pivot swing starts shut-faced and ends open. From this alone, one would suspect that neither can be the ideal basic type for the majority of golfers, and that somewhere between the two must lie the ideal.

Look for it, and who do we find but – Sam Snead! Between the two extremes we have a swing like his, in which the action is such that the blade of the club would seem to be in a neutral position all through: in the halfway-back position, in the top-of-the-backswing position, when halfway down again, and into impact.

I hope it will be seen from these few words that what may start shut or open in the backswing does not necessarily arrive as such at the top. I hope, too, that it will be seen that pivot and hand action are very closely related.

Sometimes one can change the pivot by thinking of a particular hand action, and similarly one can change the hand action by changing the type of pivot. The important thing, of course, is to decide which is the easiest for each individual. Whatever one does in the downswing must balance what has gone before in the backswing, and the whole action has to be moulded into one that is easily repetitive – for the player concerned.

Two master variations: Ben Hogan (above) swings in a rather flat plane, but gets the club-face into a neutral position at the top by slightly cupping the left wrist; Sam Snead (below) keeps the club-face in an ideal neutral position between shut and open throughout his long, flowing swing

The Left Wrist: Straight or Cupped Under?

I AM often asked, by good players, what I think to be the best position at the top of the backswing; whether to have the left wrist straight, or whether to have it cupped under the shaft.

Let me begin by making it quite clear that I think it of no importance – provided the position used fits the rest of the swing. Great players have used both positions. It is largely a question of which is the most natural to the person concerned. Some individuals can indeed vary this position at will, but others are stuck with what they do naturally.

The left-hand grip has a definite bearing on what position the hands will be in at the top of the backswing. If the left hand is put well over, i.e. showing three knuckles at address, it is more likely that the left wrist will cup under the shaft at the top of the backswing; this is so because the left thumb is more out of the way and the hand is more over the shaft, so that the wrist is more free to break across the back of the hand.

This type of grip pretty well necessitates this particular top-of-the-backswing position, too, in order to keep the blade open enough. Put very generally, a three-knuckle grip will tend itself to shut the blade of the club, but

Here are four players with different types of wrist action. From the left, Ed Furgol, Bobby Locke, Syd Scott and Bernard Hunt, showing the full range: from the highly cocked, to the flat left wrist with the thumb under the shaft

will be balanced by a complete underneath wrist-cock at the top of the backswing, which will tend to re-open the blade.

A grip, on the contrary, which has a left hand showing only one knuckle at address, will tend to stiffen the wrist-cock at the top, since the left wrist will cock *against* the left thumb – thus producing a straight left wrist at the top of the backswing. This type of grip does not necessitate the cupping of the left wrist, since the club-blade will be open enough naturally.

Generalising, then: in the orthodox type of backswing we have two distinct patterns. One with the left hand showing only one knuckle at address, usually producing a straight left wrist at the top of the backswing; and the other with the left hand much further over at address, necessitating a cupped left wrist at the top of the backswing.

Should you be the type of player who suffers by presenting the club-blade to the ball incorrectly, don't be afraid to experiment with your grip and with the resultant wrist action. Normally, if the left-hand grip is moved to the left and the wrist action stays the same, then the club-face will be more open at the top – other things being equal – than it would if the left hand were further over the grip at address.

At times, however, a left hand placed a little further over the shaft, and thus producing a fuller cocking of the left wrist at the top of the backswing, can produce a more open-bladed swing. This is often the case with players who feel that the only way to open the club-blade is to show no knuckles at address with the left hand; from this position the left wrist usually goes very flat and locks at the top of the backswing; so that, in spite of the grip, the club-face will be too shut.

Great players have, of course, used many combinations of grip and wrist action. From no-knuckle grips and a cupping of the left

wrist at the top of the backswing – which has produced a very open-bladed position requiring lots of wrist flick and roll in the hitting area – on the one hand, to four-knuckle grips and no cupping of the left wrist at the top of the backswing – which of course produces a very shut-faced position, requiring all push in the hitting area, and corresponding body action to make this possible.

The intelligent player decides what is needed, what is most natural to him to do, and therefore which is easiest to change. For example, if you naturally flick and roll in the hitting area, this will usually need an open-bladed top-of-the-backswing position. On the other hand you may have been trying to flick and roll to get the blade square if it has been *too* open.

This is where a change of grip, and therefore of your top-of-the-backswing position, may be the answer.

Conversely you may be a 'pusher' in the hitting area; in this case the blade will not need to be as open, but make sure you are not just pushing the ball only because the club face is too shut at the top to allow you to do otherwise!

I have tried to show how one must balance the grip with where one arrives at the top of the backswing, and in the hitting area. If something is wrong, try to decide which of these things would be easiest to change, to get the desired result.

Some years ago the great Ben Hogan described his personal 'secret' as a cupping of the left wrist at the top of the backswing; thus, I venture to say, he opened his club-face more than it had ever been before, enabling him to get away from the tendency towards hooking the ball, which had always dogged him before. Obviously, it was by experimenting that he found that little thing out. If you're not too happy with your own game, do try and do likewise: *experiment*.

Conscious — Unconscious

Only the hands can hit the ball, and hand action must be consciously learnt. But for the good player attention shifts to the pivot and swing of the body – leaving the hands to work automatically.

GOLF is played with the hands and wrists, I don't suppose anyone will dispute that; the club-head can only be *accelerated* by the hands, and the blade of the club must be *controlled* by the hands if it is to be consistently square at impact.

Now whether hand action is a conscious, forced thing, or an unconscious, natural thing, leaves room for argument. Some would say that the club-head is swung by the hands, and the body action follows; while others would insist that the swing originates in the body, and works out through the hands to the club-head. Now which of these two statements is correct?

Personally, I think that, as with most statements made about golf, there is merit in both points of view. The essential difference in the two methods is that in one the club-head is consciously swung with the hands, while in the other, although the club-head is still swung by the hands, this is largely unconscious.

With a beginner, who has just been taught the grip (which, to say the least, will not be too comfortable just at first), hand action, cocking the wrists and uncocking them, will definitely be conscious. Even at this stage, the wrist action will be an individual one, and will vary considerably from one beginner to another; there may be a full wrist-cock, and

to be 'alive'. Once this is established, though, I submit that the hand action will be timed much better by pivoting the body and letting the hand action follow that. Put it another way: are we going to swing the club from the outside of the circle, i.e. the club-head, or from the hub of the circle – the body?

Personally I come down firmly on the side of swinging the club from 'the hub of the wheel'. This type of action is so much easier to groove than the delicate business of open-

Gary Player told me at the 1961 Open at Birkdale, the same year in which he became top money winner on the American tournament circuit, that he believes his hand action is unconscious. Of course he has trained his hands to work for him and now he thinks almost exclusively of getting his hips out of the way to allow his hands and arms to work through the ball

consequently a lot of hand action, or a slight wrist-cock, and what looks like much less hand action. This does not necessarily have a direct bearing on how far the shots will go. With the beginner, however, hand action is definitely a conscious thing.

This really is essential in that the connection between the club-head and the body has

ing the blade of the club in the backswing and cocking the wrists, and then trying to square up the blade with the wrists at the same time as one is hitting with them.

Most of today's players have cut down on wrist action in the backswing, which has given their swings more of a 'one-piece' look, but the unwind of the hips in the downswing

67

and through the ball is actually conserving all the hand power for the hit, *rather than wasting any in swinging the club down.*

The modern players, in fact, are *not* in the classical mould of fine free swingers – as we have understood that in the past. They would seem to be much more mechanical and direct. They *are* using their hands – but not as consciously as we used to think.

Hips, too, are much more open at impact these days, which allows for the hands and arms to hit wider to the target. This gives the impression of *pushing* the ball, as opposed to wrist flick. I don't believe this is really the case at all, though: *the body is merely being used in such a way that the wrists do not roll so quickly.* Unfortunately this wrong impression of pushing the ball has been given by photographs taken just after impact; and I have taught quite a number of people at times whom I found to be trying to resist their hand action in the hitting area. This was an idea I had to correct. I submit that the good player, who plays from the hub, neither resists them, nor works them unnaturally.

We often read these days of players who play from 'open to shut' and 'shut to open'. It would be more true to say we all play from open to shut, but some use their bodies in such a way that the blade goes from open to shut much more slowly.

As the reader may gather, I am all for this type of action; but I do want to say emphatically that it is not a method which requires the hands to consciously *not hit* – any more than they should consciously hit more than they wish to! I am a great believer in hand action being natural, and in building the swing around that. Coming into the ball, one should have a feeling of the blade being square, so that one has only to hit through – not either to roll the club-head closed because it feels open, or to resist wrist action because the blade feels too shut.

Playing the game as I have endeavoured to describe, the hands will be *kept* swinging, as they are working both in the backswing and downswing. This will groove the club-head swing, and will be found more able to stand up to the pressure of the really big occasion.

Plane and Width

Numerous enlightening books and articles appear describing varying aspects of the golf swing. But there are two aspects, in particular, which rarely find their way into print.

These neglected portions of the swing are:

Plane and *Width*. Whilst it is obvious that both are closely related to other departments of the game, I intend here to single them out for the special attention they merit, if rarely attain.

Firstly, the Plane. Why is it so important? Because if the plane of your swing is correct, the angle of attack on the ball is correct. That sounds difficult. Let's look closer.

Generally speaking, a swing in the correct plane gives you *a fairly flat bottom to the swing*, which is what we want in order that the power we are unleashing will proceed directly through the ball. The same amount of power, or more power, applied more steeply,

Plane of attack. (Left) At the top of the backswing Eric Brown's hands, left shoulder and club-head are all in the same plane. (Above) Peter Thomson's legs, hips and shoulders set up the correct hand action through the ball. (Below) Coming through the ball Bernard Hunt (left) and myself are still in the same plane with the body out of the way, the right shoulder under and the right arm long

or from an incorrect plane, cannot hope to hit the ball so far.

My idea of a correct plane is one in which if, at the top of the backswing, we extend the line from the left hand to the left shoulder downwards, that line should then approximately aim at the ball.

It is obvious, then, that the plane of the swing will vary with the distance one is standing from the ball. This in turn varies with whatever club we are playing. For example, one stands close with a 9-iron, because of its short shaft; and the resulting swing is much more upright than the swing with a driver.

There is no real problem with this *change* of plane, though; for from the player's angle it is purely automatic and should merely vary directly with the length of club used.

Now in the correct pivot in the backswing there is a certain degree of shoulder *turn*, linked with a certain degree of shoulder *tilt*. One can soon deduce how a swing with too little downward tilt of the left shoulder, and too much turn, will be too flat. Similarly one with too much tilt, and too little turn, becomes too upright.

Each swing, though, produces its own characteristics. A 'too upright' arc usually makes for better iron play than wooden club play, since these iron shots are hit on the downswing. Correspondingly, a 'too flat' swing often works very well with woods, but is of little value for iron shots, since these are then hit nearer the bottom of the arc.

The present vogue is to aim at an upright swing – which I suppose I would prefer to a flat one. But why not swing *in plane* – which will then be the right degree of uprightness for all shots?

Now to deal with Width – *the relative widths of backswing, downswing and follow-through.*

This again is very neglected, but very important, and closely bound up with the plane of the swing.

Let me stress first three things:—*normally the backswing should be fairly wide, the downswing relatively narrow, and the follow-through wide.*

Read this again; for if we could think along these lines, I feel sure that this would be beneficial in governing the way the wrists and hands work during the swing.

The reader will have noticed that I said that the backswing should be *fairly* wide. A backswing can be too wide if the right elbow strays too far from the right side, due to delaying the wrist-cock too long. The backswing is best described as a swinging wrist-cock. Too much stress on the wrist-cock could make the backswing too narrow, and too much stress on the 'one-piece backswing' would make it too wide.

The narrow downswing and wide follow-through, which is the real difference between today's great players and the others, is facilitated by getting the width of the backswing right, and it is only another way of describing 'late hitting'. Something I find most noticeable among the great players is how straight the *right* arm is during the early part of the follow-through. When I see this, I know that the downswing was narrow and that the wrists have delayed their hit for the ball and not used up their power in the downswing.

Many players, unfortunately, start the club down from the top of the backswing with an uncocking of the wrists, resulting in an early, ineffectual hit, usually behind the ball. I feel it is imperative that it should be the bottom half of the body which should bring the hands and arms down to hip height. This unwind of the hips to the left, accompanied by a transfer of weight on to the left foot, will keep the wrists cocked and the downswing narrow, allowing for a powerful, late, *wide* hit through the ball.

This *wide hit through* is also very important from the point of view of accuracy, as the club-blade, bound to close after impact, will close much more slowly if the through-swing is really wide, with the club-head travelling out after the ball, close to the ground.

Summing it all up then, try to think thus.

Keep the head still, turn in plane and use the hips and legs in the downswing to help the hands hit *through* the ball instead of at it.

Timing —
The Elusive
Quality

It's the ball you are hitting, not the backswing.

MOST modern books on golf have abundant and arresting action pictures, showing positions in the backswing, downswing and follow-through. Perhaps it is this factor, as much as any other, which causes us to think of a swing in three distinct parts. To do that may be well enough – except that sometimes it can lead to the loss of that essential element in our swing known as timing.

What an elusive word that is in relation to the golf swing! One hears, so often, 'My timing was a little bit off today', when some unfortunate has had a bad day; and, as it happens to so many of us, it is perhaps not a bad thing if we try to be more specific and pinpoint this gremlin of bad timing, which can strike at the best of swings.

When it happens to me, I try to remember one thing, and often it helps; it is this: 'Remember, I want my maximum speed at impact – *not* before.'

If I can let this really penetrate my mind, it is the easiest way to cut out that quick snatch back from the ball, or the snatch from the top. When I see it in pupils, I find myself saying: 'Don't forget it is the ball you are hitting, not the backswing.' Put another way round, what I could say is: 'Wait for it'; but I think it is easier to wait for it if you know what you are waiting for! Anyone who has watched Henry Cotton *strike the ball* can sense that the backswing and downswing are no more than the essential preparation and waiting period necessary, so that the hitting of the ball can be done with the utmost authority. Remember, then, where it is you want your maximum.

One often hears that piece of advice: 'Swing back slowly'; but for my part I can't pretend there is much in it that I agree with. Some of the best players I know swing back fairly quickly. Britain's Ryder Cup Captain, Dai Rees, is no exception. Nevertheless he is accelerating at the ball. It may well be that he goes back quickly – but he comes through even quicker! So if you are not naturally a slow swinger, don't go back so slowly that you forfeit your own natural rhythm.

I have often been asked, too, how to develop a pause at the top of the backswing – possibly because it is said of me (and I believe it is true) that I pause at the top of my backswing. Well, if you don't, as I do, *naturally* pause at the top of your backswing, then my advice would be: don't try to.

Right into the years when he was playing in tournaments as an elder statesman, Henry Cotton had the power to attract enthusiastic galleries for his mastery of striking. His perfection of rhythm and timing has been an object lesson to us all

The essential thing to remember about this part of the swing is that, since there is a change of direction from upswing to downswing, it should be done fairly slowly – but never so slowly as to lose rhythm.

If you can keep in mind where you want your maximum club-head speed, I think it will help you to go over the top at a manageable speed.

Another point I frequently make to my pupils is to get them to feel that the club should swing at a speed related to the body. In other words we are *swinging*, a point so often forgotten when people become too position conscious. As I said earlier, it is all too easy to think of the swing in terms of three parts and forget that the striker in the perfect attitudes that books present to us, *swings through* those positions.

I feel sure that many of you have, at some time or other, swung a golf club starting back from the *half-way-through* position, and found it easier to make a well-timed movement from that start too. That would seem to be because the start of the actual backswing would then be fluent, and would so indicate how important the pre-swing waggle and forward press are to good timing.

Strive, then, for a fluent pre-swing movement which will help the backswing get under way. If the start-back is too slow and deliberate, then you will tend to go over the top quickly and be petering out at the ball.

Timing is elusive, because it is individual; but a swing that starts quickly enough to keep its rhythm, slows sufficiently to allow a change of direction, and comes through with its maximum speed building up to the hitting area all in one smooth flow, would surely suit most of us and help to give us good timing.

Know Your Enemies — The Four Basic Bad Shots!

As I have written before, my personal practice is not to teach a method, but to teach people. As a teacher, what I tell any individual golfer depends only on what are his own personal errors and performance. But there are many rules that apply to everyone, and in particular the basic ones of *what produces what*. To understand them is the groundwork of golf.

In a correct straightforward shot, the swing goes straight through and the blade makes contact square to the ball. In a bad shot, one or other (or both) of these things does not happen. The four simplest, and basic, errors are illustrated in the diagram on the next page.

It can be seen at once that the Pull and Slice swings are very similar, as are also the Push and Hook. Before we go any further, I should like the reader to imagine that these are the *only* four types of bad shots. There are no others which are anything but variations of these. (A socket, fluff, top and other embarrassments are only different types of near miss or mishits.)

The flight your ball is taking will always give you the clue to what you are doing wrong.

Let's take the Pull first: where the ball starts left and continues straight to the left. Straight away we know that the swing is across the ball (out-to-in), and the blade is inclined to be shut, but square to the line of swing; so that in this particular instance the swing somehow has to be swung round from across the ball to straight through. An out-to-in action is usually caused by one of two things:

(i) Insufficient pivot in the backswing, i.e. picking up the club rather than winding up the body. If this is happening, then the swing is always on an out-to-in arc, both backswing and downswing.

(ii) If the backswing is reasonably correct, the through swing can still be thrown out-to-in by using the hands or shoulders too early in the downswing, thus getting the club outside the plane early in the downswing, and consequently hitting across the line.

Should the ball be curving to the left as well then we need to make the blade less shut; so check that the Vs between thumb and forefinger of both hands have not got too far to the right; and also that the hands stay ahead of the club-head long enough to prevent any rolling of the wrists coming into the hitting area.

Let me stress again that if the shots start left and go even more left, then the player knows he is swinging out-to-in with a face shut even to his wrong line of swing.

Everything I have written about the Pull applies to the common-or-garden Slice *except* that here the face of the club is *open* to the line of swing at impact. Once again, the swing is out-to-in, for which corrective measures are the same as above. But this time the two Vs of the grip should be checked to see that they have not got too much to the *left*. If not, and the grip is correct, then the hands are not working correctly in the hitting area – usually not applying the club-head to the ball.

If the shots start left, or straight, and slice

away to the right, then the swing is out-to-in with an open blade due to incorrect grip or bad use of the hands.

I feel I must add here that most slices are due to what can be described as the body being applied to the ball, instead of the hands and arms applying the club-head to the ball. It is this that causes the club-face to be left open.

That's the basic sum of out-to-in faults – generally termed bad players' errors, because they are usually caused by too much body in the hit and not enough hands.

Now to what are generally assumed to be 'good players' faults' – the Hook and Push. Let's take the Push first.

To begin with, a true push shot goes *straight* to the right, with no curve of any description. Immediately, we know that the swing is too much in-to-out, with the blade open to the *intended* direction, but square to that in-to-out swing line. This is one of the easiest errors to eradicate, as a swing that is too much in-to-out can usually be corrected by placing the ball a little further forward (more towards the left foot) in the stance and thus having the *feeling* of hitting slightly the other way across the ball. This new position of the ball will, in fact, move the swing less in-to-out, allowing also a little more room to get the blade square, and to clear the hips.

In the Hook, as in the Slice, we have the swing in one direction and the blade in another. But there the similarity ends, for in the Hook the trouble is quite opposite, the swing being in-to-out, and the blade being shut to the line

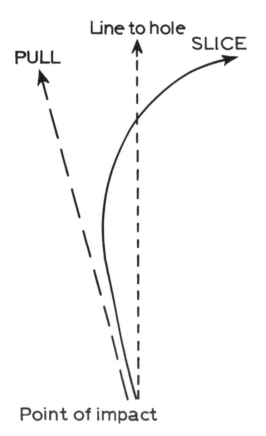

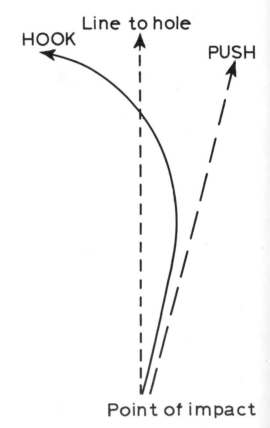

74

of swing at impact. Check that it is not an incorrect grip (with the Vs too far to the right) that is closing the blade. If you are satisfied that the grip is not at fault, then it is the wrists that are rolling and will need to be kept up with the club-head longer through the hitting area. Again, move the ball forward in the stance to help the swing to be less in-to-out, and to clear the hips, which will help to slow down the wrist roll.

I think that is enough about the four basic bad faults of golf! I hope that in future any reader to whom this is new will be able to understand from the flight of his own shots which one of the four is his own speciality. Reading the flight, he can follow up its cause with the correction, here given, and will at least be working in the right direction.

I hope so much talk of bad shots has not put the reader in a state of severe depression!

Rather, I hope he will feel more able to help himself deal with his problems. For all I have really tried to do is to give him a mental picture of what is required.

Remember, we have two things to consider: the direction of swing through the ball, and the blade position at impact.

To read one's own bad shots it is important to understand that *where the ball starts for is invariably the direction of swing, and that if it curves in its flight then the blade is not at right angles to the direction of swing*. Obviously, if it curves left the blade is closed, and if it curves right the blade is open.

Lastly, since I have talked so much about the direction of swing, the reader should bear this in mind – invariably an out-to-in swing will follow if the ball is positioned too far forward in the address just as an in-to-out swing is more likely with the ball too far back.

Causes and Remedies

Because both the slice and socket are such pernicious faults, let me try to give the causes and remedies more thoroughly.

A slice is caused by an out-to-in swing, with the club-face open to the line of swing. This action applies side-spin to the ball, which will then curve to the right during its flight.

Now the grip is largely responsible for the club-blade position, and therefore should be the first thing to be checked. If you are a

slicer, you will most likely need the V between thumb and first finger of both hands to point to your right shoulder.

Now for the out-to-in part of the trouble. The stance has a very large bearing on the direction the swing will take, back from and through the ball. The natural reaction of a player who tends to slice is to aim left to allow for it. Sometimes this is done consciously but more often it is unconscious. From this address position the club-head will start back outside the intended line; it will almost certainly then stay there, and chop across the ball in the downswing.

A bad stance thus will cause a bad pivot, just as a bad grip will cause bad hand action, and consequently a bad club-blade position.

This can also happen by aiming to the right in an effort to get inside. This causes a flatter

In these pictures I'm trying to show how a player afraid of slicing, and aiming left to allow for it, slices even more certainly. In the stance the shoulders are aimed slightly to the left, setting the plane of the swing out-to-in. The take-away is outside the line, up to a position of insufficient pivot, the club shaft pointing to the left of the target at the top of the backswing. Down in the same out-to-in plane – and the player is all set to cut across the ball again

shoulder turn in the backswing and often, in slicers, a resultant counter-turning of the shoulders in the early part of the downswing. Thus, although the backswing was inside, the downswing will be very much outside and across the ball (pictures above).

Remember that at address a line through the shoulders should point to a position only slightly, if at all, left of the target, and that the left shoulder must be distinctly higher than the right. A good grip and stance will help to get the shoulders to wind up inside on the backswing, which will get the club-blade square and inside at the top.

Now it is a question of *staying* inside when we start down. To do this the start down must originate in the lower half of the body (i.e. feet-legs-hips), *while at the same time swinging the arms down to leave the shoulders behind*. A lateral hip movement to the left, while still keeping the head behind the ball, will help to pull the hands down on the inside. From this position they will accelerate the

Here I'm showing what can happen to an habitual slicer who tries to correct it merely by aiming right and making sure of getting an in-to-out backswing, only to get into a flat shoulder turn, which is reversed at the top to throw the right shoulder round and out instead of down and under, so that he still comes at the ball from the outside

Most sockets come quite simply from an over-flat backswing, which throws the down-swing outside the line by a shoulder roll to bring the club-head two inches or so further from the feet than it was at address. A correct backswing (on the opposite page) sends the club back down and under to an accurate impact

club-head through the ball as the hips turn out of the way, allowing for a complete follow-through.

To sum up on the slice: the common cause is too much shoulder effort from the top of the backswing, and too little hand action; so *check the grip*. Too much shoulder will put the swing across the ball; too little hands will leave the blade open.

Now for the Socket: such a dreaded golfing disease that, should it strike, it often completely demoralises its victim.

The first thing to do then is to *keep calm*.

If we can do that, it is simply a matter of cause and remedy. For the socket is simply explained – the club-head is being brought down further away from the body than it should be. The ball is then struck where the shaft joins the blade of the club, and so shoots off to the right.

What causes this? Undoubtedly a flat backswing, which will throw the club away from the body in the downswing. The remedy then is to make sure that the wrists are under the shaft at the top of the backswing.

From this position the club-head will swing

sound, a feeling of *using the hands under the body* is what is required.

In deciding which type of socket one might be suffering from, remember that the right-sided one produces pulled iron shots as well as sockets, and conversely the left-sided socket produces pushed iron shots, along with sockets.

Here is what can happen if the left side so completely dominates the swing that the right hand never comes into the stroke at all – leaving the club-face lagging and open and causing another socket

down and through the ball instead of *out and around*.

What I have just explained is usually known as the right-sided socket. This is so because in the downswing the club is being thrown out by the right hand and shoulder. By far the major proportion of sockets are of this type.

There is also what is commonly known as the 'left-sided socket'. As its name suggests, this is caused by the left hand and arm completely dominating the right hand in the hitting area, thus leaving the blade of the club very open and hitting the ball on the socket that way.

The first thing to check, in this case, as in all shots produced by not having the club-blade square at impact, is the grip. If this is

Pitching and Chipping

This was obviously a difficult one, but Dai Rees made no attempt to scoop the ball. The club has been allowed to do the work in a quite simple, fluid way

ON any pitch or chip, you must have a mental picture of the shot you are attempting, before you can even choose the right club for it. I hear far too many players (particularly ladies) saying things like: 'I always chip with my 7-iron.' When I hear this I know they don't picture the flight and run of the shot before they play it.

The following diagrams, I hope, will give some idea of what I mean about choosing the club to play.

Many factors, of course, affect what picture one may get of a particular shot: the speed of the green, slopes on the green, wind, condition of the approach to the green, etc., etc. Once you have worked out the shot, select the club that will do the work most simply; then – let it. If you need a low shot to run, you will obviously select a straight-faced club: and when you need height and stop, a more lofted one.

Once you have the right club it is only a question of hitting through the ball, *letting the loft of the club you have chosen give the height and run necessary for the shot.* The hands should be slightly ahead of the ball at

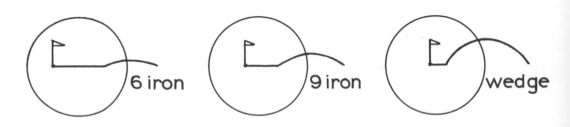

6 iron   9 iron   wedge

address and impact, so that the bottom of the arc will come just after the ball is struck, thus avoiding any scooping action, with its dangers of a 'fluff' or a 'top'.

These two foozles are often caused by choosing too-straight-faced a club for the shot you want. The player senses that the shot is going to run too much and tries to add height and stop to it by flicking the wrists early in the downswing.

Summing up: first select the right club; then let it do the work.

The Ladies

THE biggest difference in natural method between first-class men players and first-class women players lies in the way nearly all the women get up on their toes to hit the ball. There's a perfectly simple reason for this.

Not being so strong in the wrists as men, to get full power into the shot they have to start unleashing their wrists and hands into the ball earlier in the downswing than men do, in order to come into the ball at the same stage of timing. The early unleashing of the hands and wrists obviously widens their arc into the downswing and makes it more horizontal with the ground just before and into the hitting area; so that to make room for it, they have to

I have been to continental countries quite a bit for special teaching sessions. Here I was trying to help some of the promising young French ladies in 1959. Those watching include the Vicomtesse de Saint Sauveur, Mlle Brigitte Varangot, and her sister

rise up on their toes. They get their full power by slinging the club through the ball, not driving it at it.

To go with this earlier wrist-action, women's grips as a whole need to be in the two- or three-knuckle style with the left hand: that is, turned more on top of the shaft than a good man's needs to be. This gives them more power in the wrist action, which is what they need. In general, correspondingly, a flat left wrist at the top of the swing won't often suit a woman, because this itself makes it less easy to sling the club on the way down.

Unfortunately the need for free wrist action leads many women into overswinging. Trying to get power, instead of being content with a good left arm and a good wrist break, they sometimes loosen the leg action, giving the pivot no resistance by allowing the left heel to come too high off the ground. This softens the whole action, causing the left elbow to break and the wrists to go completely, and thus defeats its own ends. To get the best out of her free wrist action, a woman needs to harness it to a reasonably straight left arm and a good hold of both the

club and the ground in the backswing, or else she very easily develops an out-of-control swing which merely exhausts itself before the ball is hit.

Let's look at how a woman needs to make the most of her power. To get her hands into the ball in the timing that goes with her swing, she is going to need to hit fairly early, as I said, if not right from the top of the backswing; but once she begins to start to overswing then she will also start to hit *too* early. As a general rule, she should not start to hit (that is, to unleash her wrists) before her hands swing back to a level with her shoulders. Even then, she needs good leg action to take her swing through the ball: her leg action must be up to carrying that early hit right

In 1961 the L.G.U. sent their most promising young players for a course with me at Sandy Lodge. The girls were tremendously enthusiastic and I found it a most rewarding experience. The pictures in this chapter were taken at this course and help to illustrate the points I have made

through the ball and up into the follow-through: not getting ahead of it or lagging behind it.

It is the need for this synchronisation of the soft, slower wrist action and the swing of the legs and hips which makes so many good ladies rise on their toes in the hitting area. They really need to get through the ball and up into the follow-through with complete ease and freedom; and this is one reason why for women a good hip action, with the left hip getting out of the way on the downswing and right hip swinging firmly through with the stroke, is so important.

If there's one thing which always does puzzle me about the ladies in general, particularly the good players amongst them, it is that as a whole they are not better at chipping and putting. Being in general more delicate, and sensitive in touch than men, they would, you'd expect, excel in this part of the game where exactly these qualities count most. The only technical reason which occurs to me why they don't is simply that their natural need to hit earlier in the long

game affects, by habit, their short game, which needs a later hit. Most of them do hit too early when pitching and chipping, and consequently are not as good in this whole department of the game as they should be, on their general ability. Their general tendency is to peck the ball off the turf, instead of swinging through it and allowing the club's loft to do the job.

Generally they don't putt as well as one would expect them to, either; but here – and this probably goes for chipping as well – it seems to be a question of concentration. Most women play the game purely for pleasure. Most do not take it as a challenge in the same way as a man does. You'll rarely – outside championships – see a woman practising putting. Perhaps her performance on the course doesn't touch her pride in the way a man's does his. Golf, after all, is pretty unimportant compared to the job of bringing up a family and running a home. Yet, they love competition; in fact some of them never seem to play except in some competition or other – and they take these with a keen interest. Rita (my wife) plays in a club competition most Tuesdays, and if I am away at a tournament and ring up to tell her how I have done, if it happens to be a Tuesday I get her story before she gets mine. And what a relief it often makes from the sometimes agonising post-mortems of tournament golf!

Ben Hogan and his 'Modern Fundamentals'

BEN HOGAN'S *Modern Fundamentals of Golf* is a remarkable book in every sense; but before singing its praises I would dare to make a single criticism – of its title. Rather than 'The Modern Fundamentals of Golf' I should have liked it to be called 'My Method', for I feel this more appropriate to the context of the book.

In this book, and with the help of the brilliant Ravelli's outstanding illustrations, Ben Hogan has set down, in painstaking detail, all that he has thought, done and ultimately discovered about his own golf over a period of 25 years. I now repeat the phrase, *about his own golf*. He describes magnificently *one method* of playing golf.

Without doubt this book is an essential for every student of the game, and should be read as thoroughly and intelligently as the great Hogan has every right to assume it will be.

To me it would appear important that the reader of this book should bear in mind that it is really an 'anti-hook' book! When Ben Hogan first appeared on the tournament scene he hooked the ball; at times, he even hooked badly. He has, therefore, spent his entire golfing life perfecting a method by which, if he failed to hit the ball straight, then he was going to *fade* it rather than to hook.

This method, now, requires the back of the left hand to stay square to the target throughout the hitting area.

Not only is this the most important part of any golf swing, it is also the most difficult. If this position of the left wrist at impact can really be achieved, then the blade of the club will stay square through the ball.

Once liable to costly hooking, Ben Hogan developed a left wrist held firmly towards the hole at impact, showing only one knuckle and guarding him against any tendency to throw the club-face round. He coupled that with a hooded, low-moving club-head action and a slightly faded shot. The club points slightly left of target at the top, the left wrist is cupped to open the face and snaps back to its position through impact, holding the blade square for the fade as the swing comes very slightly out-to-in.

An easy statement to make, but unhappily, there are very few people who ever attain Ben Hogan's left wrist position naturally! For those who would like to, however, I can suggest practising: aiming left of the target with something like a No. 6 iron. This will automatically tend to make your left wrist hold up to the stroke in the Hogan position. When you can aim five yards left at 140 yards'

range and have your ball finishing, not left, but more or less on target, then you can feel your hitting area hand-action is similar to that of the great man. The blade should actually be striking the ball hooded (but not closed), that is with the back of the left wrist ahead of the club-head at impact, and the club-face correspondingly tilted slightly forward *but facing straight at your line of aim.*

This, of course, is the type of action which produces a low flying ball with a tendency to fade. The club is swung *very slightly out to in.*

There is one difficulty I foresee in all this. For most people, Hogan's grip will present the club-blade open to the ball. His terrific impact speed – probably the most impressive part of his game, and which overcomes the most likely effect of his grip with the Vs of both hands pointing to his chin, or even left of it – is for them quite unattainable; and so I do feel a grip more orthodox than Hogan's, with the Vs pointing more to the right of the chin, would suit most people better. Indeed I venture to say that Hogan's grip plus a *slow* impact speed would produce slice upon slice. (Ladies beware!)

For myself I was delighted to read that he is quite definite about what moves first in the backswing – namely *the club-head*. I do not recollect ever having read this before. In my own mind 'a one-piece start to the backswing' has been taken too far and is the cause of many floating right elbows. I have spent many an evening studying action ciné films I have taken of some of the leading players and, almost without exception, the club-head is the first thing to go back.

Ben Hogan's conception of the backswing does, I know, help many players. His idea of being in a plane does so much for all parts of the body – hips, shoulders, arms, wrists and legs – and only requires one thought to do it. He so rightly terms it a means of re-peating the same backswing, and it is obvious to us all that the first requirement of any swing is that it should be repetitive. For myself, I get pupils to swing the club at eye level to give them the feeling of swinging in a plane. The plane of the swing has certainly been more than neglected in the past.

Hogan also deals with the relative widths of backswing, downswing and follow-through: again, things which the past has too often ignored. His own 'flat-bottomed' swing allows the blade to follow-through the ball very close to the ground with the club-blade square, but hooded.

The amount of space and detail he has devoted to the waggle is a beam of light showing clearly the character of this man, Ben Hogan – the burning desire to spare no efforts in attention to detail, which eventually made him what he unquestionably was, the greatest player of his day, if not of all time.

I am not afraid to have it termed hero-worship when I state that in his presence I have always been aware that I was in the company of real greatness; and I am thankful that I was fortunate enough, on occasion, to see him play some of his greatest golf.

His composure, surely supreme, and his lightning club-head speed at impact will always come clearly to my mind whenever the name of Ben Hogan falls on my ears.

Bunker Play

To my mind there are four different types of bunker shots, which I shall deal with in the following order:

1. When we are a long way from the green and we need distance.
2. When we are bunkered near the green.
3. When the ball is deeply embedded in the sand.
4. When we are bunkered by the green and can play a chip off the top of the sand.

1. Starting with the shot from which we want maximum distance, the most important thing to do is to select a club with enough loft to clear the front bank of the bunker, *allowing for the normal impact of ball first, divot afterwards*. To ensure this type of

David Thomas (right) playing for the pin, taking only a shallow divot of sand and a full follow-through. Note the angle of the blade, held towards the hole, after an open, out-to-in swing. Henry Cotton (below right) dealing with a ball embedded in the sand. Stance, blade and swing are square and full of power and he takes enough sand to make sure of getting under the ball safely

impact the ball should be played a little nearer the right foot than usual. Selecting the correct club is so important because if there is any feeling of not being able to get the ball up quickly enough, a scooping action will creep in. This should be avoided at all costs, otherwise the wrists will use up their power early in the downswing and the club will invariably catch the sand behind the ball. Should this happen, distance will be lost. Ball first, then sand.

2. Now for the second type of bunker shot: when we are trapped by the green, but the ball is lying well. So long as the sand is fairly soft, use a sand iron. Should the sand be very wet and hard, use a No. 9 iron. Now, take up a slightly open stance, and make sure that the feet are firmly planted in the sand; position the ball opposite the left heel and hold the blade slightly open; using a fairly full swing, splash the back edge of the club into the sand just behind the ball – and *follow through*. The feeling is of pulling the club through the sand with the left arm so as to take a shallow divot of sand from under the ball. The club-blade should not dig deeply into the sand, but rather

Bernard Hunt taking one off the top of the sand from a clean lie in a shallow bunker. The hands are still ahead of the club-face at impact to avoid catching sand behind the ball. This is one where you must not look up

slide under the ball and out again. The distance is varied not just by the pace of the swing, but by taking more sand for a shorter shot than for one slightly longer.

3. Now for the ball which is buried in the sand. Obviously our main concern is to get it out of the trap. We now play the explosion shot. This time the ball is positioned between the feet, and both stance and club-blade must be square. Aim at hitting two inches behind the ball, but with more of a downward blow so as to make sure of getting under the ball. It is even more important that the feet be very well planted in the sand, as we shall need to use as much power as possible to dig the ball out. With the club-blade held more squarely, the club will tend to dig into the sand and curtail the follow-through.

4. Lastly, when we are bunkered by the green in a very shallow bunker and find the ball sitting on top of the sand, which makes it possible to chip the ball cleanly. A word of warning – don't play this one unless the conditions are really favourable. It must be a shallow bunker, as we cannot hope to get much height on the shot. A No. 9 iron is a good club to use; the stance is slightly open and the ball positioned towards the right foot. The hands should be between four to six inches ahead of the ball. Use the ordinary chip and run type of swing, but be very particular to have the hands leading the club-head at impact.

N.B. *Watch* the ball: you can't afford any head up with this one!

On the following pages I demonstrate four basic bunker shots

Ball Lying Clean – Splash Shot to the Pin. Stand slightly open with the ball opposite the left heel. Lay the club-face open at address and then swing long and slow with the club-face open at the top and the whole swing slightly across the ball from out-to-in. As you come into the stroke drag the club-head through the sand, splashing the ball out

Ball Half Buried – The Explosion Shot. Stand square with the ball half-way between your feet. Keep the club-face much more square to the pin than in the splash-shot. Swing more steeply and firmly and drive the club-head down and through the sand behind and under the ball

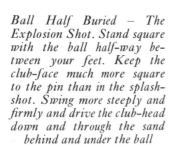

*From Under the Lip – The Cut-Up Shot. Here you need to make the ball rise sharply. Stand
well open with the ball placed outside the left toe. Lay back the club-face, swing across the line
from out-to-in and cut right beneath the ball itself*

Going for Distance. Here you want to take the ball cleanly on the club-face. Everything depends on selecting the right club and then on the accuracy with which you strike the ball. Stand with the ball between the feet, the hands ahead of the club-head and the blade square. Swing upright and keep the hands leading in the downswing to avoid hitting the sand behind the ball, and fluffing

Trouble:
To Get
Out — But How?

Harry Weetman, one of the strongest recovery players, has made the club-head do the work here by using his hands and forearms to dig the ball out of a bad lie. Despite maximum effort and the slope he is playing from, his stance remains firm. Note the toe of the club forced through along the line of aim

I AM always filled with wonder and admiration when I am on the spot to see a great player getting out of trouble. One would imagine that recoveries were things they had little occasion to practise; but it is the old story – a first-rate player is master of all the shots.

There are, of course, different types of golfers who seem to thrive on recoveries. James Braid, of a by-gone era, immediately comes to mind as one, and in contemporary golf Harry Weetman would seem to be as proficient as any. Physical ability, like that of these two players, makes recovery possible from places where most of us would soon find it beyond our strength to do more than get out. I have seen Weetman smash a No. 7 iron 170 yards out of rough when, from the same spot, I should have been content with a mere wedge of 30 yards back on to the fairway. But we mustn't despair; there is much to be gleaned from knowing our capabilities, and how to play out of trouble within our limits.

First of all, let us decide how much to attempt.

This must always vary on two counts, the proficiency of the player and the problem confronting him. Having driven into trouble, one may as well resign oneself to the fact that, usually, it is going to take two more shots to reach the green. One must see the lie, and how far away is the green, before one decides what to do; but the safest and surest way of playing it is usually, in the long run, the best. I mean, of course, that when one has a bad lie, a No. 8 iron and then a No. 5 to the green often pays off better than a brave No. 5 (which may not come off) and a No. 8 to the green. It is better to make *sure* of getting out of the rough, even if it does leave a longer shot to the green.

Often, in the rough, we are tempted to take out our No. 4 wood and have a go; if the green is in range this can be a good thing, *provided* that, if the shot does not come off, we are reasonably certain of still being on the green in two shots.

In these instances, strength, along with the

95

player's ability and the state of the game, is undoubtedly a major factor. Not all of us have an abundance of either strength or ability, so the question is how can we best make use of what we have?

I would say that, firstly, one should muster one's imagination and resourcefulness to determine what can be attempted, and how best to achieve it. If the orthodox way is impossible, one must be original enough to see

Bernard Hunt (above) found an exact gap in the trees with this shot. This is where it pays to stay down longer. Note the precision of the hands and arms and the angle of the club-face. David Snell (left) in the process of winning the 1959 Match-Play Championship, pitching from a bare lie and keeping the blade open through the ball. Peter Alliss (below) works out exactly what he intends to do with this one in a gorse bush. Whatever else, he made sure of getting the club-face into the ball

an alternative way of getting the same end-product. Remember Walter Hagen, who, finding himself confronted with a short pitch on to a very hard green, which was bunkered fore and aft, and with a gale blowing full force behind him, saw that orthodoxy was out and promptly hit the ball along the ground with his putter. The ball obliged by running through the front bunker and finishing on the green. The moral being that even had the shot remained in the bunker, he would have been no worse off than trying to play the impossible and finishing in the bunker at the back.

96

Christy O'Connor, with only inches to spare, manages to direct this back up the fairway on a straight line to the pin. Control of the club-blade was critical in this one

Recovery shots around the green need a mixture of imagination and feel. The ordinary recovery shot, from a not-too-bad lie around the green, is not normally too difficult to play when one has pitching room. It is usually a routine of inspecting the lie and deciding which is going to be the best club for making contact with the ball; we can then see what flight and stop we shall get, and pick our spot to drop the ball on accordingly.

Decidedly more difficult are the shots around the green where we are short of room. It is now when our imagination and feel come in. I must just say that if you haven't room to finish by the flag, well you just haven't room! – and will have to legislate for being past the flag. But there may often be other complications, in the form of bad lies. I think it as well to deal with these in categories.

1. *A grassy lie*. You cannot hope for much backspin, because you will have too much grass between the blade of the club and the ball, so that here you will have to choose your most lofted club and use height, instead of spin, to stop the ball. You must use a long slow swing with an open blade, which will *lob* the ball *slowly* on to the green. It's very like a bunker-shot.

2. *Grassy and downhill*. Again we cannot use backspin; and since the ball is lying upon a slope, the swing should be steeper to avoid hitting all the grass behind the ball. To get this one on to the green I suggest picking up the club (again your most lofted, usually a sand iron) and hitting down steeply behind the ball, keeping the blade open. Following through won't be easy with so much grass around the ball and with the steepness of the blow; but do try to follow through as much as possible, so that the shot does not peter out too early.

The shots dealt with above require that the blade of the club should not be allowed to close at impact, and it is therefore important that the hands should stay ahead of the club in the downswing and at impact. In both instances – particularly the downhill one – we can't hope to stop the ball quickly; so, if you have room, allow for run.

3. *Bare, but otherwise good lie*. This is where a good striker of the ball is at a great

Peter Thomson (left) pitches delicately, but firmly, over a tree. The club-blade is open and held low towards the hole. (Below) Arnold Palmer, the master scrambler, playing in the 1961 Open at Birkdale. He pushed the ball safely out on to the 16th green. The hands are still firmly in control of the club after impact

advantage and will hit the ball crisply with a lofted club, although not one with a big sole – which would bounce against the ground and cause the leading edge of the blade to hit the ball half-way up, with disastrous results! Off this type of lie, it should be sensed that back-spin will stop the ball, and the need for height is to some extent eliminated; just as well, since height is rather difficult to achieve from a lie which has nothing under the ball.

Should one be confronted with this type of lie where the green is above the player, so that height is essential, then a long, loose bunker shot type of swing is the only thing. But *don't* try this before you have practised it. It is essential that the bottom of the arc is absolutely under the ball.

4. *Bad bare lie.* For shots around the green this is probably the most difficult, and leaves one with no alternative but an old-fashioned bumble. To try to get height on this shot is courting disaster.

You will see that I have tried to explain what may be attempted around the green from the type of lies most commonly found. You have then to fit the type of shot possible into the problem facing you. How much to risk, which contours to use, which side of the hole to play for, if a straight one is not possible –

above all, *do decide exactly what you are attempting to do in the way of flight and roll, before playing the shot.*

Finally, we all find lies from which playing away from the hole is the only way to be *sure* of getting clear of trouble. Indeed *some* lies are unplayable; let's admit them and not attempt the impossible.

Henry Cotton

I FIRST saw Henry in 1938 at Sandwich, when I was a small schoolboy. He was loosening up on the practice ground, and I remember my awe at what he was doing: hitting ball after ball with a 5-iron held in his left hand only, and hitting them so consistently that his caddy was almost standing still putting out his hand for each one as it bounced.

He has probably been the most impressive striker of a golf ball I've ever seen. The only men I could possible say were his equals are Snead and Hogan.

His swing always interests me; it is most characteristic and individual. He begins the takeaway rather after the Hogan pattern, swinging the club round his right leg in the beginning of a flat arc, and opening the face quickly. But then he doesn't chase the same plane round. Just before the club-head comes to hip height, he lifts hands, arms and club into a different and more upright plane. If he were to follow his initial take-away plane right round, he would probably reach a position at the top of the backswing rather like Bernard Hunt's. But the change-direction lift he brings in sends him instead into the old

orthodox classical position at the top, with the blade open. To match this he uses lots of right-hand action in the hitting area.

He is one of the world's masters of being able to hit a longer drive when he wants to. He does this by 'hitting earlier'; that is by throwing in his wrist action from a higher point in the downswing than he normally does. In this way he widens the arc of the club-head into the ball, and flattens the bottom of its arc in the hitting area; so that the club-head is travelling parallel to the ground for longer

Henry Cotton's swing is flat away from the ball, lifting to a more upright position at the top. You can see his perfectly in-plane approach to the ball with the hands beautifully poised and controlled in their action and leverage

99

than usual, and takes the ball on the horizontal, instead of the usual slightly downward line.

When you watched him during one of his really combative rounds, you could see this happening. I remember him once at Moortown, Leeds, taking a look down the very long 10th and then suddenly hitting one in this way, 30 yards further than he had yet driven during that round. It is this sort of real mastery and artistry in his golf, coupled with his wonderful striking, which – whether they know it or not – is what makes crowds follow him even when he is no longer likely to win tournaments, and which makes him the man professionals will walk out from the clubhouse to watch – surely the most sincere compliment any player can have.

Since he last won the Open in 1948, his appearances in tournaments have steadily become less frequent; but, as I said, whenever he still appears you will always find professionals watching him, seeking to analyse or pick up something of his authority, and wonderful timing. They go to watch him, too, for his command of the difficult irons, the long irons – and to see the way he applies those tremendously strong hands and forearms of his to the game. Watch him closely, and you can not only pick up his wonderful sense of rhythm but you can actually see him hitting the ball, so definite and masterly is the stroke.

He realised early in his career that the naturally good player, as just that, was soon no longer going to be good enough; so he set to work to study the game intently. He has given it a tremendous amount of thought; for all along he has been a great applier of himself to whatever he decided to master, at each stage.

With this single-mindedness, and the responsibility of the trail-blazer, went some of the characteristics of a stormy petrel. There were times when he stuck his toes in and begged to differ from the rest of his profession, or at least from its governing body. This I have always thought was just one of the symptoms of genius, which nearly always shows its peculiar freedom in action, in decisions and in independence of speech. In early days, he never mixed much with his fellow professionals at tournaments; but he has mellowed now with the years, and to sit and talk golf with him is a fascinating experience.

Rather than being born with the ideal temperament for competitive golf, he had to master a rather fiery one. He was a puritan about his game, with such determination to hit every shot as he knew he could hit it, that any failure to do so tended to infuriate him. When he found this did not help his golf – as we all find it doesn't in the end – he set himself to control it ruthlessly, and did.

He always looks to be a bad putter; and in comparison with the rest of his game, I suppose he is. But the point really was that he missed fewer greens than his contemporaries; so he was more often putting for the hole: and perhaps he was never really as bad as his own brilliant iron play may have made him appear to be. Certainly he could putt magnificently on occasions. When I played him myself in the 18-hole final of the 1954 Penfold Tournament, he one-putted from the 7th to the 12th inclusive to kill me stone dead; and at the time it was pouring with rain and blowing like billy-o.

His influence on British golf can be counted

the greatest since the triumvirate of Vardon, Taylor and Braid; but it has been incidental to his own high standards and his determined way of life, which themselves led people to look at professionals in a different light. The value of his career has certainly been, in effect, to lift the status of the professional from that of a high-class caddy to that of a qualified man in his own right.

During his time, with him always in the van, the professional has become much more the proprietor of a business; he has become expected to be much more of an all-round personality, able to meet people, discuss clearly the principles of the game, dress well, and if necessary speak in public. In sum, he has moved right into the middle classes. With Cotton's own great gifts, his outstanding ability, his presence on and off the course, his insistence on only the best being good enough for the tournament competitor off as well as on the course, his immense flair for publicity, his writings, and his whole manner of living and the standards he set for others, he had a very great deal to do with the speed with which the general transformation has come about. The reason he has been able to count for so much lies, I think, in character: the simple fact that in whatever field he had made his career, everyone else in it would certainly have known he was there!

I sometimes feel that he might have achieved even more for his profession in general than he has done; but perhaps that itself is a measure of the size of him; and, after all, everything he did do came as the by-product of the single-mindedness of his own career. He did not set himself out to change the status of the professional; he set himself out to make Henry Cotton into the man we know today, and by his example opened the way for others.

Watch him for his rhythm. Whenever I watched him, I always played better for the few days afterwards. I remember particularly playing a round with him in the Ryder Cup trials in 1953, when he was captain. He played well and I was inspired to do so too: and I'm sure his rhythm had got itself somehow imprinted on my mind. Whenever he plays, this picture is there for anyone to get their own impression of, and try to take back into their own games.

Friends, Rivals and Partners

BOTH Peter Alliss and Bernard Hunt have had their bridges to cross. It has probably not been to Peter the great advantage everyone thinks it is, to be the son of such an illustrious golfing father. There is much expected, so early, and an unnerving amount to live up to. For Bernard a different dilemma: so little expected by people – assailed as he was on all sides about the features of his swing. I remember how furious it made one in 1954–55 to hear the would-be authorities remarking: 'Well, he could never last with that swing.'

To them both, success came early – as professional golfers go – and at 23 they had both sufficiently made their mark in golf to play in the 1953 Ryder Cup match at Wentworth. The experience of playing Nos. 6 and 7 in the singles, coming to the end in the knowledge that No. 8, Harry Bradshaw, was home and dry, and that all rested on their young shoulders, and then both missing

*Success came early to Peter Alliss (top) and
Bernard Hunt*

Alliss (above) has a full wrist cock at the top of the backswing and a lot of hand action in the hitting area. This is in sharp contrast to Hunt (below and over the page) who has virtually no wrist cock and who hits the ball more with a forearm drive

frightening little putts on the very last green, stayed with them in the two years that followed. 1954 and 1955 were relatively poor years for them both, mainly because some of the bright, clear confidence of youth had been shattered.

In spite of – perhaps because of – these setbacks, however, I have no hesitation in saying that they are both better players today than they have ever been, with a future awaiting them that promises to be as good as the present. Both now take a great interest in the administrative side of the P.G.A. Their progressive, yet sound, ideas I know will benefit the profession as a whole.

It is in the swing where the two really differ, but (and all golf pupils please note) they tell me the ways of making good pastry are legion too! The real thing is that they have both made the best of their natural ability, and then practised sufficiently to make it repetitive.

There is a major difference in their swings, which, to me, is the different amount and type of hand action they use. Accept that the hitting area consists of a certain amount of

pure flick of the wrists, coupled with a certain amount of pure push of the forearms. Then note how Peter has a full wrist-cock at the top of the backswing with a corresponding large amount of *wrist action* in the hitting area. Bernard, on the other hand, has little wrist-cock in the backswing and then a predominantly *forearm drive* in the hitting area. It is this lack of wrist action at the top of Bernard's backswing which has always made his backswing look flat.

Suffice it to say they both have a *balanced* swing; by that I mean that their respective positions at the top of the backswing are balanced by what they do in the hitting area.

Neither will lean for one moment on past successes, for both have learned tenacity on the way up. Thanks be, it is coupled with humour and philosophy; and our country can be proud that she has two such able ambassadors, who I think will represent us for many years to come.

Bobby Locke

THE infuriating undertone of condescension that seems to taint some people's recognition of Bobby Locke just leaves me aghast. When I meet it I usually begin to quote records; with such a list of successes as Locke has, though, I soon give up the long recitation and just throw in the plum – his having won the Open four times. This speaks for itself.

'Well of course,' so often comes the reply, 'it's his chipping and putting he's got to thank for that!'

Is this really the summing up Locke's career deserves? That he was without doubt the finest exponent of the short game I would, of course, echo. But his long reign of successes, before the road accident in which he was lucky to escape with his life, were based upon more than just this: he was one of the greatest golfers of all time.

Consider his driving. Few people have come to realise how good he was in this department of the game. Some years ago he broke a favourite driver, and for some little time was unhappy without it; but this short interlude was only conspicuous because it contrasted so strongly with his usual practice of missing fewer fairways than probably anyone else in the game.

Always, moreover, without being prodigious, he has driven the ball far enough. His hooky flight may be an unimpressive one to study from the tee. But this only misleads the spectator; for invariably the ball arrived in the spot Locke had picked out for it, and what else than this are we aiming to do?

Let us look at his iron play – and really it deserves a hard look. Locke has always been a very good medium- and short-iron player. He has the most uncanny ability to judge and feel the distance of these shots. In fact, after playing with Bobby, the lasting impression I always have of his shots to the flag is that of surprise – surprise at time after time arriving at the green to find his ball much nearer the hole than I had expected it to be. Why?

Because he is invariably – day in, day out – pin-hi!

If this game of golf be ball-control, as I personally believe it is, as opposed to merely hitting the ball, then it must follow that Locke's record under all types of conditions, and in all parts of the world, and over a

Locke's unique swing (left) – a closed stance, huge pivot, club shaft pointing away to the right of the line of aim and a hand action which opens the club-face. But from this position he has an impeccably grooved in-to-out swing which has won him four Opens. His putting ability (above) is legendary

period as long as twenty years, must surely be unsurpassable.

Look closely too at another department of his game. The best club in Locke's bag is his temperament! It is this ideal mental approach of his that gives him the true secret of his success, which is the ability to hit the ball the same way all the time.

This is something engineered by Bobby, and rigidly conformed to because it pays off. No one who has watched his demonstrations at golf clinics would dare say it was because he knew no other way of playing, for in these he performs all the recognised shots of the golfing purist. But in competitive golf he reverts to the style the purist abhors – because, wisely, *he knows* that this is how he best masters the ball.

Be it on windswept Scottish links or lush American courses, it is all the same to Bobby; playing the same way all the time is his recipe for success. It also gives him vital confidence. No need to try out new theories and worry about his swing – on a tournament circuit Locke is one of the few players genuinely relaxing between rounds and conserving his nerves and energy for the vital moments.

It may, indeed, be pointed out that this is a trait common to many leading players of today. Intensive practice in the earlier stages has ensured them a grooved swing; what practice comes after is of a loosening-up nature, designed merely to start that swing flowing again. Like Locke, they have learned the futility of energy-sapping or experimental practice. They prefer to retain in the peak of condition whatever swing previous practice has shown to be their most workmanlike and consistent.

One last look at Locke's placid, slowed down, strictly-under-control temperament; this time at the sixth sense that gives him his fantastic ability to read all types of greens. In general, six-footers are missed just as often from taking the wrong line as from mishitting the putt. But for Bobby to read a green wrongly is rare indeed.

Is this akin, I wonder, to the quality that gives him his reputation for never forgetting a name? For someone as world-travelled as Locke, this in itself would command respect. That it does I know, from examples I have seen; and I for one, being a quite impossible case for remembering names, would give much for a taste of this precious sixth sense in this count – to say nothing, of course, for the miracles it might bring to light for me on the greens.

Dai
Rees

ONE wonders where to start! He was there in the newspaper reports of big events when I was a small boy at school. He's a non-smoker and very nearly a tee-totaller. Nowadays he seems fitter than ever, and with more energy than anyone else. Not only does he have the usual tournament professional's busy summer, but he goes flat out through the winter too. He's the sort of man who's always got to have a go at anything that comes up; he can't bear to be doing nothing, and whatever he's doing he's got to

must be – to get by despite rather unreliable putting, as he did for some years after the war. Before the war, strangely, he was a wonderful putter, and not as good a striker of the ball as he is now. His putting nowadays, happily, is more on a par with the rest of his

Rees finished one stroke behind Palmer in the 1961 Open at Birkdale at the age of 48. Here, at the short 17th, you can see his perfect position at the top of the backswing, a characteristic one which allows plenty of club-head action through the ball

do well. He just can't bear to do anything badly either – in a tournament you can see from a hundred yards away exactly how he is going in any round by the mere look of him. He hates hitting a bad shot; and when he does – it wasn't his fault anyway! He doesn't *recognise* failure, as such, ever.

Perhaps this is partly why his record in tournaments is tremendous; he has won more of them than any man in this country. Obviously, though, this must have depended upon his ability as a player, plus his fighting temperament.

He is now a great striker of the ball. He

game, and this has helped him to stay so firmly at the top for so long, as he more and more closely approaches the age of 50.

His swing is a good sound orthodox one, with special individualities about it, arising largely, I think, from the fact that he is a small man with a great deal of strength and spirit built into him. If you watch his swing carefully, you will see that he lets the club handle drop at the top of the swing out of the grip of the thumb and forefinger of his right hand and down to rest in the V between them. For almost all ordinary golfers this would be a hugely dangerous habit; but with him it has

What a tremendous competitor Rees is, always pushing the club up firmly at the hole

always worked, and may easily have become necessary through his lifetime use of a two-handed grip, with no overlap of the fingers as in the usual Vardon grip. The effect of dropping the grip into the V like this is to make the club-face slip into a very open position at the top of the backswing. Certainly the position at the top makes, *for him*, a wonderful one from which to give the ball the biggest cuff with the right hand, which is just what his temperament tells him to do, anyway! It is so regular and grooved now that he manages to be a very straight driver with it. (An odd corollary of this habit of letting the grip slip in the right hand at the top is that he can't play his best with tacky grips, which don't slip easily – the very reason for which other people like them!)

He is probably the straightest driver amongst British professionals. He has got the idea into his head that he is; and when he has an idea he lives it! He hits remarkably few crooked shots, anyway.

His greatest métier has been match-play golf – despite a wonderful record, running back over many years, of close tries in the Open. He has played in every Ryder Cup match since 1937, and in 1961 captained the team for the fourth time, winning one of his foursomes, and both his singles.

One of the secrets of him is that he never gives up. As, indeed, his record in the Open suggests, he is the most magnificent rear-guard-action fighter (typically, he came back to within a stroke of Arnold Palmer at Birkdale in the 1961 Open after Palmer had taken an almost impregnable lead a few holes earlier). The Open indeed he has had a good chance to win on numerous occasions: and certainly a man is unlucky to have come so near so often yet never to have made it. Of course, if he had managed it early on in his career, he might easily have won it more than once. A really big target that you can never quite hit eventually gets a sort of hoodoo on it for you, and this may have happened to Dai with the Open. Certainly no man who has won the Match Play Championship four times, as Dai has, can be said to be not good enough to win the Open.

I think the great example and object lesson he offers to the tournament watcher is simply his fitness. He drives a Jaguar over 20,000 miles each year, gives countless exhibition matches, and is an indefatigable after-dinner speaker.

In sum, he's really livelier than life: and long may he continue!

Norman
Von Nida

I PARTICULARLY wanted to say something in this book about Norman; because the public over here seem to have a very wrong impression of him, largely due to the bad treatment he used to get from some parts of the Press here. He is really one of the best of men, and one of the most likeable too, amongst all professionals.

Of course he was always highly strung. He put everything he'd got into his game; and at times – caring so much how he played – he could be explosive. When he felt the Press

A perfect hitting position which somehow shows the small Von Nida's immense determination to match – and beat – the bigger men

were getting against him, maybe he decided to play them at their own game! I remember one occasion in particular when he was trying to hole a five-footer before a huge crowd on the 3rd green at Hollinwell. Every time he got down to the putt a man in a car behind the crowd started revving up his engine. Norman backed away from that putt three separate times, then he very slowly walked across the green, parted the crowd, and walked slowly up to this fellow sitting in his car – and he tore him off a really gigantic strip. And he'd every right to! The man hadn't thought whether anyone was playing the game! But in the next morning's paper, of course, Norman was slated! Maybe you or I might have talked with a little more forced politeness. But that was not Norman's way; he came right out with it – just as he would have said it to one of his fellow Australians! And the same would go when he was interviewed later. He wouldn't say deprecatingly: 'Well, this chap *was* revving his engine...' Not a bit. He'd describe the man exactly as he saw him!

Another characteristic example of his outspokenness was when he came to stay with me in Egypt and found that my wife was not a member of the club. Normally – in those days – a professional's wife would join the nearest other club very often. But there wasn't another there. There were a lot of people, even then, who didn't agree with the old practice of not letting the professional's wife join the club (in fact, since she couldn't use the club swimming pool, the British Ambassador gave her a permanent invitation to use his private one at the Embassy, whenever she liked). I never spoke to Norman about this. In that match-play championship he was beaten by one hole in the most wonderful final by Hassan Hasanein, who went round in 66. It was really wonderful golf and everybody was very excited about it. But at the prize-giving Norman spent one sentence on the golf, and the better part of half an hour haranguing everybody about why the heck the club professional's wife couldn't be a member! I've never felt so embarrassed in all my life! I just didn't know what to do or which way to turn. The next day I had to go and explain to the secretary that I hadn't put him up to it. But that was the sort of fellow he was! If he felt there was wrong being done he'd take all the cares of the world upon him; and strangely enough people – including those club members – always seemed to take it well in the end!

He was just the same off the course. If he ordered a cup of tea in his hotel, and after half an hour it hadn't come, he went and sorted them out! And what's wrong with that? I sometimes think the rest of us should follow his example more closely.

He was, in this, typical of the Commonwealth in many ways, particularly in that he said exactly what he meant the whole time. A lot of people misunderstood him in that, but he always was, in fact, a very fair person.

All the time the Press was rather building him up as an explosive trouble-man, his fellow professionals had a very different idea of him. We all always liked him. Even a young assistant, come out of his club for the first time with a swing with which he couldn't break 90, could go straight up to Norman von Nida and ask his advice – and get it – even when he was right at the top of the tree, even when he was in the middle of winning a tournament. We all respected him.

He's a most courageous person. When he first came over here, in 1946, he hadn't much in his pocket when he went down to Wentworth to practise. The professional there, Archie Compston, quickly got him into some money games, which he took on with the greatest alacrity – despite the fact that if he had lost them, he might have been in real trouble!

Accepting his chances, and playing them his own way, goes for his approach to golf in general. He's never been the sort of man to play the same shot all the time. Rather he is a purist and always plays the shot which is required, in complete contrast to Locke. If the fairway dog-legs to the right, then Norman will fade the ball from the left-hand side; if he stands on the fairway and sees the way into the green is not exactly straightforward, say for instance that the green be tightly bunkered short and left, then he'll accept the challenge and draw his iron shot into the green from the right. At his best, he always played the shape of the hole. He could do this simply because he was a great striker of the ball, and always felt he could command it to do what he wanted for him.

There was an immense amount of hard work behind his game too. He was, when at the top, a tremendous practiser, not just before a tournament or at the beginning of the day, but even between the third and fourth rounds of a tournament he was winning, he'd still go out and hit balls. He was fit as anything, and tough as only an Australian can be.

He was a grand player for several years, and always a courageous one. He never wilted in the final round. He was a great trier. There was nothing sloppy about his thinking or his condition or anything. When he won the Masters at Sunningdale in 1948 he was paired with Flory van Donck, who was leading the field by a handful of shots with one round to go. He got one stroke back and took the honour and then – I know this because he told me about it – he calculated that if he could fade a long drive round the trees straight on to the 11th green, then he might get two more in one hole – always a fair chance, there, since the penalty of going for the green and failing to make it is so often either to fade behind the trees into trouble or to go straight across the fairway into the woods the other side. Anyhow he worked out that to catch Flory, he had to do it. He could hit a long drive then, despite his size, by getting right into the back of the ball, after widening his backswing with a downward swing of his head and shoulders on the way back. He used to sink to the backswing, and then stretch to hit the ball. It was his way of getting the length of a bigger man. In his heyday, in fact, he was pretty long from the tee.

Well, on this occasion he did make the green, for his 3; and of course Flory tried to follow him, cut his drive out behind the trees, and took 5. That really put him in reach of Flory and finally he got down in two from the bunker beside the 18th green to be round in an almost incredible 63, and take the Masters right out of Flory's hands.

In his method he not only went down on the backswing to widen his arc, as I said above; he also used a lot of hand action, with the same idea of getting maximum power from his small – if sinewy – frame. It never went further, though, than a normal full cock of the wrists, and lots of club-head action. At his best he was a very fine player indeed, and a good one to look at. He was a wonderful pitcher and putter and holer out. Nowadays I still play a lot with him, and from tee to green he's still a wonderful player, but on the green his nerve's not what it was, and the short putts escape him too often.

Above all, Norman is a very generous person. For instance, both Gary Player and David Thomas, when they were on the way up, have stayed at his home in Australia for weeks and weeks, and used it like their own. He'd be up at 7 o'clock in the morning and out with them on the course; and taught them for hours – and of course he knows a *lot* about it.

He'd always want to help anyone. So often I've been playing with him in a fourball, and one of us hasn't been playing too well, and he's just taken whichever it was on one side. He wouldn't wait for an invitation. If he saw anyone doing anything wrong, a youngster for instance, on the tournament circuit, he'd walk straight over and without any ado say: 'Lad, you'll never hit it that way.' Nothing would stop him from helping people. Over here, on the contrary, we tend to be too reserved, and don't like butting in on people. I suppose I do it as much as anybody; but in general we're a bit shy about it. Not so

Norman. If somebody needed telling something – he'd tell them; and that went for his whole way of life, as a matter of fact!

I remember when he stayed with me in Egypt for the Egyptian Match Play Championship. On the last day he came to my shop and said: 'Which is the best player amongst your caddies here?' I told him, and he turned to the boy and said: 'Well, here you are, Sunny Jim', and handed over the whole set of clubs he'd played in the championship with. Just like that. Most of the rest of us, let's be honest, would have said: 'I don't want to air-freight these over to England. I've got a new set waiting for me over there. Suppose you give me 70 per cent of the value of them?' But not Norman.

He had a reputation for wildness when he was younger. But he's always had one of the biggest hearts in golf; and nowadays, when he's mellowed a lot, far more people are able to appreciate it. As I said, he'd help anyone who genuinely wanted to get better. Of course he's now very well placed with at least one manufacturer in Australia, so he has plenty of opportunity to do that sort of thing; and it's a great tribute to him that the firm concerned will take his word for any young player's worth instantly and absolutely.

Another example of his eagerness to help was in the 1956 Open at Hoylake. I wasn't playing very well, and told him so. It was 8 o'clock at night, but, 'Out we go, then', he said. We went out on to the practice ground, and he gave me a long lesson. Then the next morning he came up to me and said: 'By the way, this driver will suit you better than the one you've got', and handed me his own driver, the one he'd used the day before. There was no saying no to him, of course. I took it – and drove much better too. It wasn't in the end quite right for me completely, and I think Bernard Hunt ended up with it. No one ever paid anything for it, of course. It came from Norman, and that was the sort of effect he had on people.

People haven't always been very kind to

him over here. But I can say just this: he's been the most generous golf professional I've ever met.

Nowadays he's very happily married, with two children. He brings his wife over here whenever he can, but when he can't, he's just longing to get back to her – and he's ringing up Australia about every third day.

Peter Thomson

I FIRST saw Peter when he came to play an exhibition match at Gezira during his first trip out of Australia in 1950, with Norman von Nida. He was then 17 or 18; he had been travelling by air for a day and a half. Going straight on to the course, he understandably found his game slightly uncertain. But he was so determined to put on a show that, despite the nappiness of the greens, he managed to get down in one putt on each of the first seven holes to keep a good score going. Here obviously was a young man with some genius for the game, I thought; to have so much self-control at that age seemed to me most impressive. He was not only stale from flying, but obviously out of practice; yet he got round in 67. What most impressed me was the way it was done. First he preserved the score by chipping and putting; then gradually played himself back into form again, hole by hole, to complete the round well.

Peter has what is probably one of the simplest swings in the game. He swings the club-head back first, with a quick break of the wrists, and keeps the right elbow hard down all the time. He has, in fact, developed his own particular grip and backswing, rather shut-faced from the bend-open of the wrist break, as opposed to any roll of the wrists. He puts the club-head behind his hands at the beginning of the backswing, and keeps it there until after impact, swinging back and down again with his hands, arms and club-head in a constant relative position to each other. The narrow backswing and downswing makes him hit the ball very late and very low. This possibly explains why he is at his best in the Open on golf links in a wind.

He has not done so well in American as he has here. This, however, is a very relative statement. By all normal standards he has done very well in America in the small amount of time he has played there. On their courses you have to flight the ball higher from the tee to get distance on the lush fairways. His drive goes normally so low that he has at times dispensed with the driver, and he has actually won championships driving with a 3-wood.

If he had been a different sort of wooden-club player, he wouldn't, of course, have been such a good iron player, since the type of wooden-club swing he uses is very much that of an iron shot; and he often plays his irons, in fact, like great elongated low pitches. With this low trajectory, on running Empire courses, his secret is his almost uncanny accuracy in placing and running the ball into the right part of the green. Where a high shot,

The Thomson wind-up is in many ways a model – shoulders fully turned with hips and legs resisting. Note the very slightly shut club-face, governed by the flat left wrist. (Below) On the greens he always manages to hole the important ones

on these sort of courses, may bounce off line, his beautifully controlled, rifle-like irons hold their line on the run almost infallibly; and he can direct them where he wants them; this comes from the touch, judgement and instinct of years of playing them all this way.

In play in tournaments, he is one of those people with a wonderful even timing – helped to preserve by the simplicity and easy repetitiveness of that swing. This is underlined by the fact that he plays the *important* shot better than anyone usually hopes to. I recall him being one down to John Panton in the 1954 Match Play Championship, coming to the 18th. He took a long, long time over his second shot there; finally he played the perfect stroke to seven feet from the flag, holed to save the match, and then went on to win on extra holes. As a sort of corollary of this (and unlike Cotton) he hits more bad shots than most others in his class: but again, after each of the five or six he may hit in a round, when he comes to the next one, which really counts, he sizes up the problem he's earned himself, very carefully, and is always likely to bring off just the shot he needs to recover himself. If he is driving badly, as he sometimes does, he will still hit his irons straight to the stick. In many ways, his game is absolutely tailored for winning championships.

Peter is another great student of technique. When he's over here he occasionally comes out to Sandy Lodge, and we hit balls together and talk about method. He and I agree very much on the importance of getting set up to the shot correctly before you can hit it properly. Occasionally, when off his game, he himself manages to 'get in his own way', by misplacing his body, left shoulder too far forward in the address; and knowing this perhaps makes him all the greater believer in paying particular care to this part of the game.

The great lesson, I suppose, his game has to suggest lies in the way his hands work; that it really isn't necessary to 'go back in one piece', as we've been told to believe so often. With his club-head-away-first action, he makes a wonderful example of the swinging wrist-cock in the backswing followed by uncock in the through-swing.

He's not only a naturally tremendous player, but has almost a perfect kind of build for the game – thick, strong and not too tall. He also has the temperament to be placid on the course; during the final holes of a championship he'll never seem to turn a hair. He can, in fact, keep his head when the last run-in to the tape is on. In the last round of the 1955 Open at St. Andrews he had a horrible 7 at the 14th, but he followed this straightaway with a great 3 at the 15th. This is so often the mark of the man who has it in him to win and win again.

Perhaps one of the most instructive things about him for the ordinary tournament watcher is his short game. If there's anything unusual required of him around the green, he'll always get the ball up to the hole somehow. He seems to be able to conjure up a wonderful mental picture of how the shot is going to work; he can see the flight and roll exactly as he needs them. And of course, once on the green, he is equipped to make the most of his chances. He is always, above all, a good holer out. There again, he'll nearly always hole the important putt – the one that really matters.

Gary Player

I FIRST met Gary at St. Andrews in 1955. He played a practice round with John Fallon and myself, and I remember thinking he'd got the Hogan mentality. The round was one long series of genuinely interested questions: 'How did you do that one, Mr. Fallon?' and: 'How do you play this, Mr. Jacobs?' He kept watching our shots and trying to learn how to produce them. He obviously had a burning desire to get to the top, and was going to waste no moment in learning all he could about how to get there.

His method then was not quite what the stylist might recommend. Fear of hooking which had given him a grip with the left hand so far to the left that the V was outside his left

Ross Whitehead, Gary Player and George Low with me in 1956 when Gary was still very much the aspiring young man, terribly eager to learn all he could. (Below) By sheer hard work and study he has nowadays become very long off the tee

shoulder, and a very flat left wrist at the top. He swung at the ball very much from the inside, and stood to hit everything from right to left.

Since then he's never lost his burning interest in the technicalities of the game; that day in 1961 when we were rained off during the Open at Birkdale, we went back to our hotel, sat on the bed and talked theory for three hours.

He told me that for him the body movement is the most important thing in the golf swing, and at that time was thinking as he swung through only of turning the hips through the ball.

We professionals all have our gimmicks at any moment. Swings don't change much, but our thoughts do. You'll think for up to four months at a time of whatever you suspect to be your current weak point, which is in due course suddenly supplanted by another, which you then try to think about in its turn.

Gary will never be afraid to try something new. In that 1961 Open he went through all the practice rounds with one particular putting method. But on the first round of the Championship proper, he suddenly felt it wasn't going to be good enough, and promptly changed to another.

Gary is a disciple of Ben Hogan, both the method and the man, and has as a result of his chosen mentor adopted his slightly cuppy left wrist at the top, which has made him more upright and less shut-faced than previously. He reminds me particularly of Hogan in the way he approaches the game; he plays golf with the same burning desire to win *everything*. The bigger the occasion, the better he is likely to play. At the age of 25 (as I write this in Autumn 1961) he is still leading money-winner of the year on the American tournament circuit, with Arnold Palmer, who lies close to him. All the tournaments he has won have been the big ones, with big prizes. He's won the United States Masters, was runner-up in the U.S. Open, and began this season by taking the largest-prize tournament on the winter circuit.

Since he first went to America he has learnt to hit the ball much further. Over there there is usually lots of room from the tee; so, being a small man, he hits the ball as hard as he can on most drives.

Gary and I have played a lot together since 1955. In 1956 we practised together in Switzerland, knowing that soon afterwards we were to play each other in the first round of the *News of the World* Match Play Championship at Walton Heath. I taught him all the time out in Switzerland, and he beat me at Walton Heath. Then the following winter, when we were both in South Africa, I wasn't playing well, and he taught me solidly for a week – after which I beat him in the final of their Match Play Championship. It was an unusual example of how friends help each other as a matter of course.

Gary is tremendous fun to be with, and still very boyish. He has no inhibitions at all about performing in public, and can do a magnificent take-off of Elvis Presley. His

Player is now very good in all departments of the game. You can see in this picture the control implicit in his approach to a critical shot

showmanship is just an expression of himself too. I suppose he does do some things he regrets – the trousers he sported one season with one leg black and the other white were one of them – but in general if he wants to do something, he just does it. To his great credit he is just as natural and likeable today as he was when he first came to this country as a boy, very eager to learn, in 1955.

Recently Gary has published a book which, because he dared to say that he thought most British golf professionals were lazy, came in for a certain amount of criticism. Personally I think it is a book which every aspiring champion, amateur or professional, should read, in the chance of picking up some of his complete dedication.

About Myself

I CAN'T remember starting golf. It was just part of the life I grew up with. I suppose I held a club as soon as I was able to walk.

When I was born in 1925 my father, Robert Jacobs, had already been professional at Lindrick, near Sheffield, for six years. Later my mother became stewardess, so from my earliest moments I lived in the golf world. My father, who died in 1934 when I was only 9, had suffered ill health for many of his last years, and therefore had played very little with me. I always suppose, though, that he must have given me the right grip and stance. I seem to remember that, like most schoolboys, I was more fond of cricket and football than golf; but golf was there all the time at home and I used to play a lot, including the summer evenings. My schoolmaster once asked me pointedly: 'How many nights a week do you do prep and how many times do you play golf?' to which I answered: 'Well, I play golf every night of the week.' The rest of the answer he must have known without being told! By the time I was about 14, at any rate, the game had become an important part of my life. I used to play occasionally with my mother, who was then a good 14 handicap, and I was already playing with the local artisans, whose club I represented in matches when still a schoolboy.

Lindrick is a lovely golf course, and is always in perfect condition, with most

A picture of myself in 1945 when I was still in the R.A.F. and playing little golf

wonderful greens. I took it for granted, of course, but I loved it. You had to hit the ball very straight there, which in those days I couldn't; so that although one day I would play well and score in the low seventies, the next day I'd often find myself running out of balls.

In 1948 I tried for the York-shire Professional Champion-ship, tied with John Fallon and lost the play-off. (Below) Gezira, Egypt, 1956. Was this the fore-runner of the American golf buggy?

My father had been succeeded as Lindrick professional by my cousin, Jack Jacobs, who had joined him in 1924 as his assistant, and who is still there. My mother had stayed on as stewardess; and so things remained until the war began. I was still at school, of course, and it was not until 1943, when I was 18, that I joined the Air Force. I trained as flight engineer on bombers, and finished my training in the week the war ended. I was mad about

this at the time, but I've been glad ever since. I enjoyed the Air Force, though, and made a lot of friends. It was probably as good a time and way to grow up as any, and I have never regretted the experience at all. In fact, nowadays, I still meet old friends and acquaintances of those days. Quite recently one of them came up to me during a tournament, after following me round. I recognised his face and was glad to see him; we got talking about old days, and some of the things and people we remembered in the squadron we had both been with. 'Do you remember', I asked him, 'that riotous squadron leader of ours, who was such a good hand at a party after those cricket matches. . . .' or perhaps I used a stronger, more affectionate and colloquial phrase of R.A.F. times! A slow smile came over his face, and slowly he took his hat off. It was him, of course! – he was as bald as ever, and I hadn't recognised him with his hat on.

When I was demobbed in 1947, at the age of 22, I went as assistant to Willie Wallace at Hallamshire – having applied for the post without much hope of being taken very seriously against the many more experienced applicants. Wallace, once assistant to J. H. Taylor at Royal Mid-Surrey, was a really fine club-maker. He passed some of his skill on to me, and after I had been there a year I could face, shaft, lead and grip six woods in a day. It was an excellent training; in fact, all my two years with him was an experience I'm very grateful for.

It was there that I began the teaching which has since become such a large part of my life. I had never tried to teach anyone before, but I soon found that people began to come back to me. I seemed to be able to help them; so, although I was not more than usually interested in it at first, the problems of putting over the game of golf to the ordinary club member began to fascinate me.

The terms on which I was engaged were typical of those days, and perhaps not without historical interest for the future. I was paid £3 10s. a week; and my teaching brought in 5s. an hour, of which 3s. went to Willie Wallace and 2s. to me. For any lessons after 6 p.m., though, the whole 5s. went to me. I was soon booked up from 8 to 10 hours daily, and every evening in the summer from 6 p.m. to 9 p.m.! I used to go home at night with a pocket full of silver, feeling like a millionaire. I suppose in the summer it all came to about £10 a week; but the winter, when it was dark

in the evening, was, of course, a very different story.

At any rate, in January 1948 Rita and I felt able to get married. She had come to live at Lindrick, where I still stayed with my mother during the winter months; I lived in digs during the summer. I had, incidentally, no half day at all (I wonder who would be prepared to take a post under such a condition nowadays); it was a full seven-day week. I remember leaving home at 5 a.m. one Christmas Day in order to be there at the usual time.

Before I definitely turned to golf as a career, I had been playing to a handicap of 2. I was never really an amateur, because from early on in life I used to accept tips from members for giving them a game, which

Hassan Hassanein was my co-pro at Gezira – a great player and a natural gentleman

strictly put me into the professional ranks. At Hallamshire I really began to work on my game, and I got the first boost to my confidence when I tied with John Fallon for the Yorkshire Professional Championship, finishing ahead of the then most powerful players in Yorkshire, Arthur Lees, Frank Jowle and my cousin Jack. I went round 36 holes in 144; John, however, beat me in the play-off. It was a strange coincidence that eight years later I was to be his partner in the Ryder Cup match at Palm Springs, when we won the only foursomes point. How well he played too! He played his game and allowed me to play mine with never a complaint at any of my wayward shots. Winning a foursome point gives such a boost to one's confidence for the singles on the following day, and I am therefore particularly grateful to John for the 1955 Ryder Cup Match.

At Hallamshire I played at or worked at golf every daylight hour, but it was all a good life. Chances of a club professional's job in this country were not too many then, and obviously Rita and I were beginning to look towards getting ourselves more firmly established in the profession. So when I saw an advertisement for a full professional's post at the Gezira Club in Egypt, I put in for it, again without much expectation of getting it. Within a few weeks, though, I had been interviewed in London, accepted, and asked to take the next boat. We actually caught the boat with only one day's notice, and arrived in Egypt with only £10 in my pocket.

Out there life was a new experience. Gezira was a large club, with a vast membership, and a rich one. I was in charge of the shop, and I found business with local agents was on a sale or return basis, which helped us through the first months. Very soon we were able to get the shop going to the level we wanted, and that side of the practice was well worth all the effort we put into it, or, I should say, Rita put into it!

There were three assistants, all Egyptians, and my co-professional at the club was that

My three Egyptian assistants all concentrated on playing or teaching. (Below right) The amount of teaching that I did left me with a very flat swing

outstanding player, Hassan Hassenein. Like the other Egyptians, he was entirely occupied playing and teaching. His death in an accident at his home was a great loss both to Gezira and to golf in general; he was a natural gentleman and a great player. In 1951 he came to England with me, when I went on leave, and we played in tournaments together. In his very first tournament, at Worthing, he ran off a 66. He was perpetual Desert Champion in Egypt – an event played on a course out by the Pyramids – and to this he now added the French and Italian Open titles. He was a good man; I liked him a lot, and we all missed him after his tragic death.

At Gezira, before very long, my own main concern again became teaching. The Egyptians' enthusiasm for it had to be experienced to be even imagined. I began by teaching from 8 a.m.; but the demand for lessons from the hundreds of members soon became so pressing that I had to ration them! No member was allowed more than two half-hours a week, and no lessons were bookable more than one month ahead. The result was that every Monday morning there formed outside my shop what we called 'the mink-coat queue' – from the number of rich lady members who joined it, in the cool of early morning – though other members sent their chauffeurs to book for them.

Soon Rita and I had achieved what we had come for, a little financial security and a flourishing practice.

Life was good in many ways. We lived in a flat in a most pleasant area on Gezira Island, with a huge Arab called Hassan – he was 6 ft. 5 in. – to cook, clean and look after us. The climate was wonderful, almost always sunny. But with all the time devoted to teaching, I found my own game getting very rusty indeed, especially as after a day out in the heat I was too tired to practise in the evenings and keep up to scratch that way.

Just when everything seemed to be going really well came the time in 1951 when Egypt abrogated the Treaty with Great Britain, and

the political trouble began. It was no fun at all. We were at the club on that 'Black Saturday' when, in retaliation for our soldiers endeavouring to keep order in the Canal Zone, with its inevitable loss of life, the mob broke loose and set fire to over 300 shops, businesses and houses of various kinds, including the Turf Club and Shepheard's Hotel. The Egyptian army had to be called out to quell them; and when we heard rifle shooting over the course, we came back at top speed to the clubhouse and hoped for the best. It was an unpleasant time, altogether.

In February 1952, we just had to get out, losing all our goodwill, and a great deal of the stock in our shop. But we had enough capital, now, not to have to rush into a club post at home; and I determined to spend the summer playing in tournaments in order to get my game back.

This proved to be one of the most important decisions, and one of the most important years, of my life. I played in every British tournament that summer. At the beginning I was plainly very bad; but I spent every spare moment on the practice ground at Lindrick (for the courtesy of which, though I had no formal connection with them now, I was tremendously grateful to the club), and towards the end of the season all the effort began to bring results; I finished in the first ten in the Spalding Tournament at Worthing at the end of that year.

I felt then that I was ready to take a club post; and in December I was lucky enough to be offered the professionalship at Sandy Lodge, near Watford in Hertfordshire, where we have both been very happy since. The course is a good one, on sandy sub-soil, fairly open, but demanding enough accuracy to score well for it to be good practice. The clubhouse and members are all one could wish for. My mother retired from stewardess at Lindrick in 1955 and now is an invaluable help in running my shop. There is, too, a really large practice ground, right in front of the clubhouse; I keep an average of two

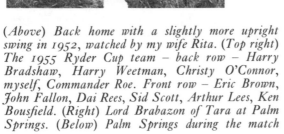

(Above) Back home with a slightly more upright swing in 1952, watched by my wife Rita. (Top right) The 1955 Ryder Cup team – back row – Harry Bradshaw, Harry Weetman, Christy O'Connor, myself, Commander Roe. Front row – Eric Brown, John Fallon, Dai Rees, Sid Scott, Arthur Lees, Ken Bousfield. (Right) Lord Brabazon of Tara at Palm Springs. (Below) Palm Springs during the match

playing and teaching assistants, and altogether it is a situation I always feel I can leave behind with a peaceful mind when I go off to play in tournaments.

It was in the season after I joined Sandy Lodge that I at last really began to do well in tournaments. In 1953 I won the Southern Section qualifying rounds for the Steward Goodwin Tournament at Sonning, with two 70s. With that, I felt I was now on the brink of being really established in my career; and to add to it, I was runner-up in the finals of the same tournament, at Lindrick. I did quite well in the Match Play Championship, too, losing to Max Faulkner on the last green in a semi-final at Ganton. He went on to beat Dai Rees the next day. There was rather an amusing finish to our match. Max was 2 up with 3 to go. At the 16th I hooked my tee shot, and then had to play down towards the first fairway outside the big tree that stands on the left of the 16th. I was nowhere near the green in two and my third shot finished 30 yards from the stick, just off the green. Max was on in two good shots and the whole match looked over. I was studying my chip when I noticed Max obviously signing the card for the marker, as if the match was already over. I went across and said: 'I saw you, Max. Well, now, I'm just going to hole it!' Impossibly, I did! Then at the 17th, with Max dead in two out of the big bunker on the left, I gave him another surprise by holing for a 2 from just through the green. But he made no mistake about his 4 at the last, and there was nothing I could do about that. That year, too, I was asked to join the Ryder Cup team trials being held at Wentworth, under Henry Cotton's captaincy. We all played six medal rounds, and I thought I played rather well. I didn't get in the team but at least I now had some sort of reputation as a player.

For the next Ryder Cup match in 1955, the team was picked on the season's averages. I managed to get into it, and went to the match at Palm Springs. I had been granted leave of absence from the club to tour over there the winter before, which proved invaluable experience. It stood me in good stead in the Ryder Cup match; because I found that, although I was very nervous for a couple of holes, I then enjoyed every minute of it. John Fallon and I won our foursome against Chandler Harper and Jerry Barber, and then I had a splendid match with Cary Middlecoff and was thoroughly delighted to manage to hold him off and win.

When I said that the tour in America had helped my golf, I was thinking of a lot of things. First, perhaps, the atmosphere of American tournaments. The United States professionals were very friendly indeed, quick to make a visitor feel at home. They all seemed to be trying to help each other all the time, and were much more open to suggestion from each other than perhaps we are over here. I remember Ted Kroll sitting in a deckchair all one afternoon trying to help me with my game as I practised in front of him.

Then, too, you learn over there to adapt yourself to varying conditions, and adapt yourself quickly and completely if you are to compete. Some courses are quite unlike anything over here. In Texas and Arizona, for instance, on the winter tournament circuit, the greens are of very coarse grass indeed, and very slow to putt. Heavy watering gives them a surface rather like an upturned scrubbing brush, while the fairways, by complete contrast, are dry and sandy.

I remember one unusual incident there. I was driving from the Bing Crosby Tournament at Pebble Beach across the desert to Phoenix one night at 2 a.m. with the late John Pritchard. Each competitor in the Bing Crosby Tournament had been given a bottle of whisky. We had put them down on the back seat. Suddenly our headlights packed up. Since we had not much further to go, I began driving on sidelights, uncertainly in the half-light, along the white line in the middle of the highway. There was little other traffic and, in any case, plenty of time to see anything coming by its lights. What did suddenly arrive

Sandy Lodge was a proud club in 1957. T. S. Waddell, our captain (centre) was Hertfordshire Amateur Champion. The American, H. Ridgeley (front left), was runner-up. J. Harrison (back left), D. J. Morris (back right) and D. Brew (front right) played for the county and I was Dutch Open and South African Match-Play Champion. (Below) With good friends Dave Thomas, Bernard Hunt, Ken Bousfield and Peter Alliss at Sunningdale. (Right) A group of competitors and friends at Gleneagles

behind us, however, was a policeman on a motor cycle. He looked at the bottles on the back seat, and then looked at us with, it seemed, the gravest of suspicion. Very soon he had me out of the car and walking along that white line myself. Luckily it turned out that he not only knew golf, but had played it in England during the war; so the affair blew over amicably enough. The bottles, at least, we were able to point out to him, were both unopened – at least until he arrived.

In the winter of 1956–57 Rita and I toured South Africa with Bernard Hunt and his wife. We played in five tournaments, and I was very happy to win their Match Play Championship at Houghton, beating in succession Trevor Wilkes, Harold Henning, and then Gary Player by 2/1 in the 36-hole final. Bernard and I played over thirty exhibition matches, and I don't think I have ever seen such a fine exhibition of iron play as he put up then. He didn't miss more than five greens in all the thirty rounds. This, to me, always seemed to be the time he began to play really well, as he has ever since. Those exhibition matches were an experience in themselves. We were travelling all the time, and usually we had never seen the courses

before; yet we had to go straight on to them and put up some sort of a show – for that was what we were there for. Our judgement of distance improved tremendously; it had to!

Back at Sandy Lodge I was teaching all through the year, and becoming increasingly interested in it. People began to come to me from some distances, including the Oxford and Cambridge teams, a number of Walker Cup amateurs and other internationals, many of the keener young amateurs from round about, and latterly, of course, both the E.G.U.'s and L.G.U.'s schools for promising young players. I met ex-King Leopold of the Belgians and have several times had the privilege of going over to stay with them and help the whole family with their games. They all play well. Their immense keenness on the game makes it very easy and comfortable to be with them, talking golf endlessly, when not actually playing or teaching.

I have, though, taking the wider view over the recent years, almost regretted a little bit becoming so much in demand as a teacher, while still young. Teaching does most certainly interfere with your own game. Although my long game stays much the same, without constant practice I soon find I don't pitch, chip and putt as well as I should; and teaching all the year round makes practice time hard to find. About 1957 I got very discouraged, and turned much more to teaching. But I now feel that when I reach 45 – I'm 38 – I don't want to feel that I took to teaching too early, and never really gave the playing of the game a chance. So nowadays I try teaching as much as possible for the six winter months of the year, and as little as possible during the summer. This is where a good staff and an understanding club is essential.

So far as the game goes, I do have another difficulty which dogs me – my legs. If a golfer's legs are not absolutely reliable, and strong enough to stand any amount of hard work, then he can hardly play his best when it matters. My particular trouble has been varicose veins. In the winter of 1954 I underwent an operation, and the following season I played well. But the old trouble slowly came back, and in 1959 I had them taken right out; I find this has been a great success. When teaching, I can avoid too much standing about by using a shooting stick whenever possible. One has to train oneself to use it, however; I take one out religiously every day but usually find at the end of the day that I have never sat on it.

The tournament field in Britain is now well worth the effort of taking part in and keeping in form for. Rewards are running higher every year, and have so far increased more quickly than competition has toughened. So in 1960 I made an attempt to come back into the tournament game, and not without success. At the end of the season I came third in the Ballantine Big Ball Tournament at Wentworth, and then second in the Masters at Sunningdale, taking £700 in two weeks. You have to stand teaching an awful long time to do that!

Whatever efforts one may make, though, to limit one's teaching and put more time and effort into tournaments, the fascination of helping people remains strong. Once you get a reputation, you begin to get better and better players coming to you, and then the thrill of seeing them going from your hands to win big amateur events and make their way into international teams. One should never perhaps underestimate both the pleasure and the usefulness of helping them to do that. I hope I don't.

Am I An Agitator?

I WONDER how many British golfers caught the glimpse shown to us by television in November, 1959, of the Eldorado Country Club, during the Ryder Cup match. Those who did must surely have gasped out loud at this spectacle of opulence and magnificence. I didn't, quite; but only because in the last few years I have seen similar show places in many parts of the world.

These are the products of the post-war boom in golf overseas, and it is natural and right . that those who are building should build with the times; the last word in décor, up-to-date facilities, well-oiled services and the like.

The same renaissance is not, you will have noticed, sweeping the British Isles, although 'loss of development' claims are responsible for the improvement of a number of club-

houses in the recent past. On the whole we seem to be paying the penalty for the fact that the first popularisation of the game was some 50 to 70 years ago.

In many cases what were thought fine adequate clubhouses at the time they were built, are now beginning to show a sorry face to their relations built in countries where golf is newer and richer than here in Britain. Let us, of course, be proud that in these islands golf is a game for all to play, not just the wealthy (anyone – and this I do believe – who wants to enough, can learn the game here). Nevertheless, it is somewhat exasperating to think that wherever one plays golf outside the British Isles one has usually not far to travel to find amenities far surpassing those we put up with at home.

Perhaps it is time we stopped laying the emphasis on economy, tradition and 'atmosphere', and made greater efforts to move with the times.

The British craving for understatement recoils, I know, from an atmosphere *too* lush, *too* pretentious, *too* smart; 'Heaven save us from *that*', the cry rings out. I have heard it from childhood and believed it for years! Now, though, my feelings have changed, and

126

I remember with pleasure the comfortable lounges, the efficient and abundant showers, the tempting through-the-day buffets and other up-to-the-minute facilities enjoyed at golf clubs, for the most part, *outside* my own land. Am I alone in wistfully wanting more here? I don't think I am, however often one hears: 'But it wouldn't go down well at *this* club.'

To install adequate heating, bright clean floor-covering and showers aplenty that really

so limited. Snacks available all day, anything from a sandwich to a quick steak, would surely be more sensible – and better, I'll warrant, for our digestions – as well as spreading the load on the courses. No reflection here on our stewards and the good fare they produce; but to me it would seem that to offer less, when it was asked for, would be a more sensible form of club catering.

Let's now take a critical look at ordinary British courses. Three loops of six, or two

This is my own practice shelter which I also use for lessons in rain or bad weather. I had it made on wheels so that it can easily be moved about as the ground gets worn. I have certainly found it one tremendously good investment

do work – is this asking too much? One really wonders.

It all goes for meals too – but in almost a reverse way. We have long suffered, and now still accept, the regimental catering habits a golf club imposes. Even through short winter days, most clubhouses put on their two-, three- or four-course lunch at the rigid time of 12.30–2.0 p.m. Everyone eats at this time, usually well, and often too much to play golf on; and everyone rushes to the first tee to begin a cold, slow round chafing behind the stream. Why we don't have snacks for lunch at our golf clubs I simply don't know – particularly in the winter when golfing time is

loops of nine holes would seem to be an obvious need, but doesn't seem to have been thought so when the majority of our courses were laid out. Never mind, it is always great fun for the golfer to ponder on what could be done with his own course; and in many cases, where the layout is not convenient, I think, a few minor alterations could easily improve it. Need it change the character of a course if it is truly a change for the better? The advantages of two or three starting points are too obvious to us all.

Whenever a course's *condition* is mentioned, expense is thrown at one from every side. But if your course is at all on the heavy side it is surely money well spent to get rid of the worms. No one enjoys playing on mud, and green fees will soon improve if you can offer the visitor a drier course than his own. Perhaps, incidentally, I am old-fashioned, but I have usually found greens treated with compost, produced at hand, superior to those fed on chemical fertilisers.

Once outside Britain one finds that 95 per cent of the courses boast a practice ground, invariably equipped with cubicles from which to hit balls, be the weather at all bad. Here it much more often is bad; but one can hardly decry the lack of cubicles when the lack is rather of adequate practice grounds at all! Few clubs today in Britain have a really good one; and even at the tournaments one usually finds that, if there is such a thing, it is (mostly) inadequate and rarely allows space enough for getting down to improving one's shot-making. As for the member who leaps out of his Monday–Friday harness only to find a course bulging at the seams each weekend – where is he to go?

Let us all agitate for better practice grounds. (It is no personal thorn-in-the-flesh, this, for my own club has an excellent one.) Let us have cubicles, too, some day. If we want them enough, there are always ways to improvise them. A roof from the rain, a cheap oil stove – how the professional would welcome it all! So many of our present winter lessons are cancelled for bad weather; and practice becomes just another way of keeping warm, not the pleasure, aesthetic and physical, it most certainly can be.

While we're about it, why not put a bunker near the corner of the putting green? It is next to impossible to learn how to get near the hole from a bunker unless you are doing it on to a green.

The professional's shop can be all or nothing. Some I have seen that are really something. A lot depends on the pro, but the club can give him a start. Too many wooden huts exist today that sufficed our grandfathers in their sales of tees, peppermints, gutty balls and the odd handmade clubs. Since the advent of trolleys, a section of these wooden pavilions is often confiscated for storing them. What remains must be stretched to fit a trade that would have scared our grandfathers to death.

Many professionals sit back and accept it, glad of the excuse to say: 'Well, what can I do with this?' Some could do much if the pros' shops were a source of pride to the members; but today it is much more likely to need the same overhauling as most of the club-houses do!

Am I really an agitator?

I think not. But it is all taking so long, and we are becoming more and more content to let it. It's a matter of money, I know, but it's more besides. Need we really be the poor relations to our golfing friends all over the world?

In Britain we have the cheapest golf of anywhere. But surely it is false economy if our golf facilities, though cheap, are classed as second-rate!

The Pro's Pet Aversions

I AM not a candidate for that school of 'Angry Young Men' said to be flourishing in England today. Rather, I am a fortunate member of that minority group lucky enough to be following a profession planned from boyhood days. But I have read the views of several writers listing the 'common' faults of our profession, and think it just might not be unseemly to retaliate with a few aversions similarly distasteful on this side of the track. Personal to me, of course, but I don't doubt that they prickle the skin of some of my colleagues too.

In first place, because it needles me most, is the modern Press, which in certain quarters only reports the 'incidents' rather than the golf. One section of the national Press only talks of the personalities and never reports the game. The greater portion of this reporting is based on half-truths and only stirs up trouble within the game. I state categorically that I have sometimes read, 'John Jacobs said . . .', when I have not even been interviewed. I suppose everyone who is in the public eye, even in a very small way, has to put up with this; but I don't see why they should. The 'tiny' putt 'nervously missed' (quote) that I know for a fact was a near seven feet and curly at that, also annoys me. That there are certain golf correspondents well qualified to comment and discuss the technicalities of the game I am well aware; one only wishes other reporters of lesser golfing calibre would stick to reporting golf. In their defence, we must add, however, that many of our national daily newspapers find golf, as it is played, dull reading for the public taste; hence, sensationalism is introduced, even into golf, often at the expense of fact.

Aversion Number 2 concerns one specific type of well-wisher – the 'on-the-spot' man. He is not to be classed with the plain well-wisher, whose support and encouragement we all need and take heart from. I am always helped by kind words and wishes from any sincere source. But those who cannot resist speaking to me whilst (sometimes even because) I am in the public eye, only succeed in exasperating. Surely those who really wish us to give of our best under pressure can understand that they may break important concentration and create disastrous distraction by coming forward at such times to claim our attention.

Every professional must like to hear, 'Hope you do well', before he does battle; few of us appreciate, 'Hope you're doing well' – because we're still *doing* it! Both remarks may be well meant, but the difference is timing. A tournament round invariably sees a professional at his unsociable worst; and it is sad for anyone to be given a curt rejoinder to a well-meaning remark. Better save it for later.

If a player *is* rude, this will worry him, as he knows it can hurt someone's eagerness to get into the picture, and may well add a shot or two to the professional's card.

All this sounds ungrateful, and whatever I write many readers will think that a few words *cannot* hurt anyone. 'Well, who do they think they are?' they might say. But if a player is known by the crowd, there can be fifty or more people thinking precisely this, and acting accordingly.

There are obviously some players who *can* chat all the way round; but, be assured, they are exceptions, and most players prefer to be left to start conversations if they want it that way, and loathe having to kill one at birth.

Number 3 we all of us know. He's the chap who has stood by your ball and now walks a few paces to meet you. Yes, you had an idea you might be in trouble and a glance at his wide happy grin confirms it! Just how bad is the lie you can tell by his glee when he eagerly says: 'You'll have a job with that.'

Number 4 is the gallery classic. An eminent personage in golf plays an unexpected bad stroke – after all it is always possible – and: 'I can do that', jeers the man in the crowd. He usually gets his applause – and then one would love to take this character aside and point out that golf is a game of percentages. The better the player, the fewer the mistakes,

know only too well how many varying factors sway the balance of success and defeat, and 'having guts' is only part of it all.

Enough of tournament trials. To close I'll stay nearer home. Professionals, like myself, today are trying to do three things as well as they can and then term the whole 'being a golf professional'. They must play the game, teach the game and run a fair business connected with the game.

In all the three departments of his job, then, standards are ever rising, and there's

Professionals vary in their reactions to friendly spectators during play in a tournament. Occasionally I like to chat when I am competing – but I like to choose whether I do or not. This picture was taken during the 1957 Masters tournament in which I came third

is the simplest of logics. It's the score at the end that speaks for itself – can the onlooker boast: 'I can do *that*?'

Number 5 is akin to 4. That hackneyed phrase, that gets in one's hair just the same: 'He's got no guts.' A derogatory summing up, usually on some unfortunate who has failed at the last fence. Equally often put forward by someone who has never cleared enough fences to have a go at the last one. Those who have,

little similarity between his business of today and that of the same business some thirty years ago. It is therefore a great advantage to be allowed to plan one's day. I try daily to allot a specific portion of my working day to each item, and in this I am fortunate in having an understanding membership to help me.

I add my next aversion reluctantly, because it no longer happens to me. I know it to have been born of the misguided conception that practice is mere filling in time. I refer to the statement made whilst one tries to practise: 'I see you are not doing anything, so may I have a lesson?' Need I say more? Only this: wouldn't it help everyone if golf lessons were treated as appointments and booked through an engagement book as one would with one's dentist? A golf professional will always be asked to have a quick look at someone who is 'off' and suggest a quick remedy if he is near at hand; I think this is his duty and privilege. But it is very frustrating not to be able to hit shots because of a small contingent who are waiting to interrupt.

I have spent a long time on No. 6. So briefly to No. 7. The odd people one teaches who, whenever encountered after a lesson, greet me with: 'Haven't hit a good shot since!' – in spite of my knowledge of a few half-crowns won in the meantime. I have even had it said in a lesson, when a really rock bottom shot has been reached: 'Now look what you've made me do!' Such pupils are not at all common; perhaps they are only remembered because they are rare. I like pupils to take 100 per cent credit for good shots, and expect it to be the same with their bad ones!

I have a last aversion: to some members of P.G.A. committees who for innumerable years have never made a progressive step. Good men, I know, but never an *idea*, not even a bad one, because they can't risk it being unacceptable. The advent of young blood has already brought into existence an assistants' training scheme, a teaching committee, and a lot of new ideas not all of which are good, but some of which will prove useful.

All these aversions may be unacceptable to the reader! But I state them, very conscious that most of them are quite innocent, inflicted without any desire to hurt or do harm whatsoever.

A Woman in the Pro's Shop

I CAN only assume that those of us who play in tournaments do so with the hopes and good wishes of the clubs from which we come. This assumption stands, however, on one very important factor – the adequacy of the staff we leave behind.

I maintain that the first responsibility of a playing professional today is to ensure that a staff sufficiently adequate and capable of fulfilling his duties remains in his absence for the convenience of his members. Even with good intentions, this is not always what occurs; and I should like to write more about this, for it is a contemporary problem for the modern golf professional, and one that never arose for his predecessors; it is the product of an ever-increasing world-wide tournament circuit.

My own first stipulation for a really good solution to it would be – and this entirely without flippancy – 'Get a woman to lend a

My mother was stewardess at Lindrick for many years, played to 14 handicap, and now brings all her experience of golf to the managing of my shop. I am sure that a woman can see to all the subsidiary details of a shop better than the professional and his assistants, leaving them to handle advice on clubs, but otherwise free to teach, practise and play

hand'. I have been to clubs when the pro has been away and found his shop closed. I know that he has one, two or sometimes three young assistants; but they are teaching, playing or somewhere on the practice ground; and the shop meanwhile is closed, which is obviously most unsatisfactory from every point of view.

I condone this practising. Any young assistant worthy of his salt will want to spend much time on it. It is always the first thing to be noticed when the shop is closed, however; and the best solution to this, I feel, is to employ a woman to help in the shop. It is not always easy, even with two or more assistants, to ensure that always one or other is available

for attending to customers, and I consider myself very lucky that in my own shop my mother takes over. I know my two boy assistants are equally glad, for – let's face it – they didn't any of them come into golf for sales experience, although it is something they must acquire.

Many duties, moreover, entailed these days in the successful running of a pro's shop, can be done much better by a woman than a man. Display, tidiness and cleanliness, and the keeping of stock in tip-top condition are just examples. The days have passed when a shop constituted a few clubs, balls and some waterproof shoes. Today we sell all types of sportswear from nylons to hats, fashion-right woollens and waterproofs, shirts, a large range of shoes and gloves, and an assortment of countless sundries and sweets. Anyway, who can sell to a woman as well as another woman? Certainly not I!

It is true to say that I personally sell most of the clubs at my club and, contrary to popular belief about professionals, am quite willing to split any set if desired. I encourage a prospective buyer to try out and hit balls with whatever he fancies, and customers are invariably advised by me as to what suits their game best.

This part aside, most sales in my business are carried out with the feminine touch. My shop is open all day and every day regardless of weather or season, for the convenience of my members. But when at my club, I myself am as free as any of my assistants to teach, play or practise – and still have some time over for sympathetic listening to a member's disastrous hole. The latter cuts both ways, for after a disappointing tournament I am glad to have time to tell any member about it and be consoled and listened to in my turn!

There is yet another side to a professional's work. Each week between forty and fifty letters go out of my shop, and a large number of parcels. Anyone running a business can appreciate the time needed today for ordering stock and returning orders incorrectly made up in size and colour. For example, a ladies' 5-iron is urgently needed, is telephoned for or even telegraphed for, and an all-weather grip is

specified. Delays in club deliveries are common, so we are not surprised when it arrives five or six weeks later – *with a leather grip*! We appreciate the golf trade have difficulties on their side to contend with; but it does all add up to more time and work which a playing and teaching professional cannot give, and which therefore in my case falls on my staff.

Air tickets and travel arrangements for a long circuit of tournaments and exhibitions are also left to my mother – a secretary as she appears at times to be. They are all jobs needing patience, tact and even, at times, ingenuity, and I should not like to have to entrust them to a boy who is itching to get out and hit balls!

I doubt if my requirements of a staff differ from those of other playing professionals, British ones at any rate; so perhaps my case for a woman in the shop may be of interest to some others.

In my own case I am indeed fortunate, and I doubt if I could replace my particular 'secretary'. I am sure my members, as well as my assistants, have found it as congenial and successful an arrangement as I have done.

Professional Standards

I FEEL confident that we shall get stronger in the international field. Now we have a small number of professionals who play golf for a living; about six or eight of them. When we can get that up to 15 or 20, we should win the Ryder Cup when it is played in this

country. We are never going to be able, on the other hand, to support 50 or 60 professional golfers just playing tournaments for a living. Nevertheless, the effect of the trend of tournaments towards better rewards and stiffer competition is improving the standards of general professional play. Every year, the standard gets better, largely as a matter of reacting to bigger prizes, etc.

The whole reason for a club pro's job, on the other hand, is to be at his club, looking after his members. He might play in tournaments now and then, but what we want is a prize list to make everyone have to try hard, to get in the first 30, with four or five prizes for encouraging the under-25s. A long prize list of small rewards encourages a lot of people to play in tournaments who shouldn't! We can only afford to encourage people who are going to help us internationally, and very few others.

It should, too, be done on a very fair basis. A man who wins a tournament by one shot, which may be luck, often gets £1,000, while the runner-up gets £500. This is up to the promoters, who want four-figure publicity. But the truth is that for the good of professional golf, I would far rather see something like £700, £600, £500, £400, £350, £300, £250, £225, £190, £180 . . . down to a £20 prize for 30th, and *nothing* for anybody else.

We are, in fact, coming towards that sort of attitude. Promoters are taking advice on this sort of thing. The big first prize, however, is their way of ensuring advertising value in editorial reports.

Any promoter of golf not only wants to get advertising for himself, but also is trying to do something for golf. Only in the recent past has it been explained to promoters that the way prizes were distributed in the past did no good. If I felt that I couldn't get in the first 30, then I should cease to play in tournaments, and everybody else should accept that, too, I think. We need smaller fields of 50 to 100 really good or potentially good players. A player shouldn't expect to play in a tournament unless he is likely to do well.

We professionals must strike a balance between being fair to competitors and giving the public what they want. The public, of course, want, and ought to have, more match play; but it isn't the best way of finding the best player. Round-robin match play is nearer to it, but still not the fairest thing. The fairest way, from the players' point of view, remains a four-round medal.

Match play round-robin, being a terrific thing for the spectators, and for the interest of newspapers and public – jaded perhaps with the normal run of tournaments – must certainly be taken in. A round-robin field, though, is very small, and we should face squarely the best way of choosing which players shall compete in it, since on any system the numbers are limited. Obviously the promoter has a right to his own say; but what the P.G.A. should aim at, perhaps, is a fair system of basing the right to take part in any invitation tournaments (like round-robins) on the general showings in ordinary open medal tournaments, which must provide the basis for all other tournament qualifications.*

I think myself that the winning-points system of qualification for things like invitation tournaments of any description and for the Ryder Cup side is preferable to any system based on averages. It is performance that counts, and that includes the pressure of the occasion and what you are trying to do. In match play and medal events alike, points should be awarded on the finishing list. I should suggest 100 points for the winner, 80 for the runner-up, and then more gradually down to no points at all for the 21st onwards.

It would, note, be a positive qualifying system. A bad performance would merely get you no points – it wouldn't actually penalise you. Others might pass you in the list as it then stood, but you would not drop down below someone who had not even competed. I should say, too, that rather than having a minimum number of tournaments to count, you could merely let all major P.G.A. tournaments count, invitation or otherwise, since invitation tournaments would be invitation by previous performance. A player would never be in danger of having to calculate the odds of playing in one or two more than the minimum, for fear of spoiling an already good average.*

A basic list of 30 major tournaments (about 15 of which would be four-round medal, from which one could decide the leading players for invitation and small-field events) should

* Since I wrote this, the Esso Round Robin Tournament has joined the list, and for the 1963 Ryder Cup match, the P.G.A. adopted the winning points system.

be quite enough to provide a living for 15 to 20 full-time tournament players. This would avoid flooding the season with so many similar events as to bore the public and – that vehicle by which the public is kept informed – the Press. In all considerations of tournament planning, you have to balance the needs of the promoter and the interests of P.G.A. members with the need to keep the public interested.

Another useful way of doing this would be to introduce more 36-hole invitation tournaments, at weekends, in different regions, but always strongly local in interest. In this way, too, the standard of national tournament golf could spread itself the better amongst the golfing profession in general; and many amateurs who have no time to watch tournaments, let alone travel to them during the week, would have their opportunities on one or two weekends in their own county.

Organisation

Everything I am saying, of course, implies a pretty good standard of organisation, initiative and good public relations by the P.G.A.

In addition to the P.G.A.'s Secretary, sooner or later as this business expands, there will have to be also a Tournament Organiser or Manager who would see to the planning, running and administration of all tournaments, balancing the points of view of public, promoters and players alike.

There should really be no difficulty about this. The P.G.A.'s income from tournaments is already big enough. Every competitor pays entrance fees, and the players have in 1961 agreed to give up also 5 per cent of the total prize money towards paying for the P.G.A.'s responsibilities.

I'm sure the time has come for we professionals to think seriously about taking full responsibility for seeing that everybody gets the maximum possible value and entertainment from the money.

The P.G.A. and the Press

The Press does as good a job as the P.G.A. allows it to – at least so far as the interest of professional golf goes. In the past, I don't think our organisation has been anything like free enough with information; nor has it accepted responsibilities for seeing that the Press have good enough facilities at tournaments. The golf writer cannot do his job properly if he has to waste time overcoming unnecessary obstacles to prompt and reliable information.

First must come a comprehensive system of telephone or wireless communication on the course, to bring back to the Press Room all the information which those writing running accounts for evening newspapers, etc., need so badly. A score-board, up to date hole by hole, is the minimum requirement. The more correspondents, not least those tied to the Press Room sending running news reports, can know about what is happening on the course, the better. And, of course, even those who walk miles every day watching play, and write full and informative accounts in the major dailies, cannot possibly be in more than three places at once (though some of them have developed a quite remarkable knack for anticipating the right moment to be watching the right player); for them a reliable means of checking what they have not themselves seen and may or may not have heard about, would vastly add to the ease and ultimate efficiency with which they could do the job. It is very much in our interests, as professionals, that tournaments should get the best possible – and accurate – publicity.

The Outlook for the Club Professional

One can sum this up quite simply by saying that the club professional has got to be much more of a businessman than he used to need to be. To make the most of his opportunities, he is going to have to stock a far wider variety of goods and types of each goods than he does today. Even now in 1963 the average professional in a small club may have a stock worth well over £2,000, and keeping this up to date calls for continual letter-writing, telephoning and hard work at detail, particularly since there are such delays on certain items of stock. Nowadays you can't sit back and wait for business, just hoping to sell whatever you've got in. You have to react to what people want, anticipate swings in

colour, quality, or even for something you haven't thought of stocking before.

On top of all this, the days of casual lesson giving are over. Golf is booming, and if a professional is to make full use of his time, his lesson-book must be booked ahead, and the only time he is not giving a lesson or playing should be when he is busy on something else. There is increasing demand, too, for lectures in the evening.

Golf is booming and the professional must use all his initiative to accept its challenge. Evening lectures are now more and more part of the opportunity he should welcome. I enjoy this sort of thing myself, as here, where I was talking to the Golf Circle of the Institute of Practitioners in Advertising

demand, see opportunities for selling things which people need and would like to be able to get in the pro shop, for meeting individual demands for something in a special size,

The modern professional must, of course, be a good teacher. Sadly, perhaps, he need not any longer be a fully skilled clubmaker, but he must be able to carry out or organise all types of running repairs immediately. Above all, though, he must have business ability and salesmanship. Even the best player or teacher in the world is going to need that all the time, especially when his more physically-active days are over.

I think myself that, looked at from this point of view, the possible value of a career as a golf professional is opening up opportunities which people have not yet fully realised. Certainly the majority of professionals themselves – especially those brought up and versed in the old traditional wooden-shed ways – have not themselves yet made the most of their chances. Playing ability is not enough in itself for a club professional any more; he has to have initiative. I can already foresee the time when the professional without initiative will begin to find the competition, from those who have, too hard for him to go on the same old way. It may prove hard for one or two, but it will be for the good of the game, and for the million-odd amateurs who play it in these islands.

Large Ball: Small Ball?

I AM firmly convinced that it is high time we came into line with our American friends and conceded that theirs is the better-sized ball to play golf with. Those who insist that our weather conditions make this out of the question should realise that it certainly blows, too, in Texas, on America's Pacific coast at Pebble Beach, and certainly on the Atlantic coast at, say, Atlantic City. It is true, of course, that in high winds the larger ball is more difficult to control, but the good player will devise means of getting performance out of it, just as racing car designers are getting the same performance from a $1\frac{1}{2}$ litre engine that they used to get from a $2\frac{1}{2}$.

Let me deal first with the 1·68 in. ball as it affects the good player in normal conditions. The first thing that stands out is that the larger ball is *not* shorter, or at least so imperceptibly as to make little difference at all, in actual play. This I think was proved by the

Arnold Palmer's left wrist at impact is similar to Ben Hogan's. The large ball calls for this driving effect as opposed to flicking

first Ballantine Tournament – played at Wentworth in October 1960. The course was playing longer than when the Daks Tournament was played there in June of that year;

These two pictures of Ben Hogan show how the hips and arms are kept moving so as to drive the ball forward. On the opposite page you can see the greater amount of hand action I use for the smaller ball

yet both the winning score and the 10th place score were better in the Ballantine than in the Daks. The real point is that if the large ball is not quite 'middled', then it flies considerably less far than the small ball does from the same sort of stroke.

To me this is a good thing. I think it may be the reason why the best American players use an action which keeps the club-blade squared for longer in the hitting area, as opposed to the more common method in this country in which wrist-flick and roll have been over-emphasised.

This type of 'blade square for longer

through the ball' we call 'driving the ball'. I think it is a more reliable and certain method of play than the flicking type of method. The large ball makes this action almost a necessity, since it tends to climb too quickly if it is not driven squarely out with a longer right-arm through the ball.

This, I think, would appear to be the essential difference between how the leading U.S. players play compared with our best players. *Generalising* then, *we* flick the ball: *they* drive the ball – and I am absolutely certain in my own mind that to drive the ball is by far the sounder method. To get results, the U.S. large size ball *has* to be driven; and therefore, right from the start, it encourages a sounder method.

Recently I read an article in *Golf Digest* by

the American professional, J. Victor East, about the Walker Cup matches, called 'Why the Americans beat the British'. Whilst I think this article slightly exaggerated, I have to admit that I agree wholeheartedly with its principles. Here are some passages from it:

'The only sound reason for American dominance is style of play. . . . The British system is not as effective as the American method. . . . The British generally employ considerable local and independent movements of the hands, wrists and forearm as they start the *backswing*. Having thus misled their muscles on the backswing in this manner, the typical British player must attempt a variety of split-second compensations on the downswing in an effort to return the club-face squarely to the ball. . . . This necessarily complicates the swing as a whole. . . . The American method keeps the club-face square to the line of flight during all parts of the swing. This is the familiar "one piece" swing so often advocated by U.S. teaching professionals.'

To my mind there exists this decided difference in style of play which Mr. East – although obviously generalising – describes. *The point which I wish to make, however, is that the style of play has been encouraged by the larger ball.*

The larger ball inspires confidence in the good player too because it is undoubtedly easier to manoeuvre. That is, if one wants to cut a shot – or hook one for that matter – it can be done with more certainty with the larger surface to work on for applying the desired spin. For the same reason, it is easier to apply backspin with the shots to the green. In short, for the good player, then, the larger ball encourages square authoritative hitting. Nothing, in my opinion, would do more to improve our best players, both amateur and professional, than to change to the larger ball. Shots to the green from a 6-iron down can be hit decisively at the flag. So often we are more concerned with holding them back so as not to go over the green.

In this country today Bernard Hunt has the type of hitting-area action with a square blade all the way through which would be encouraged by this change-over.

For the poorer player, on the other hand, the advantage seems obvious. The first thing of importance is to get the ball airborne, and assuredly this is an easier feat with the larger ball. Once this initial stage is over, it is true, as I have explained, that the larger ball does require square hitting even more than the small ball; but this very fact would, I think, encourage more correct application of the club-head at the beginning of a golfer's career.

I can't help but think that the balance of pull to slice amongst poorer players in this country is heavily stacked in favour of the slicers, and I think it is thus fair to state that the larger portion have an open blade. My visits to the U.S., on the other hand, have given me the impression that the balance over there is much more even. This means then that as a national characteristic the club-blades of American golfers are much more neutral than those of ours. This could be because the average American handicap golfer doesn't have to worry too much about getting the ball into the air. Slice-spin (or any spin for that matter) is magnified by the larger ball; therefore open-bladed shots, on a ball that tends to climb more than ours anyway, are the most affected.

The 1·68 in. ball needs hitting forward squarely, letting the loft of the club do the work. And as it sits up and asks for this with every club in the bag, it is surely easier to drive it forward than to be thinking of rolling the wrists.

I am very much inclined to believe that the weekend golfer would, eventually, find it an easier ball to play with, and one which would sooner or later automatically improve his game.

Trends in Equipment

SURELY the easiest way to play this game is to use the same action for all the full shots. Now the way good players do this is to have the hips leading the hands into the hitting area. This, of course, is what is commonly described as late hitting. I myself am not convinced that many sets of clubs are designed for this type of hitting.

It is surprisingly common for a low handi-cap man to come to me and say something like: 'I bet you won't be able to do anything with me. I slice my woods and long irons, and hook my short irons. How do you work that one out?'

He doesn't realise how common his trouble is; there must, in fact, be many people who on reading or hearing something like that would say: 'Why, that's just about what I do, come to think of it.' The explanation, I'm sure, is in the way almost all sets of clubs are designed.

The simple fact behind it all is that with a comparatively straight-faced club, like a driver or long iron, you are hitting the back of the ball more than the underside of it. As a result (other things being equal), if the hands

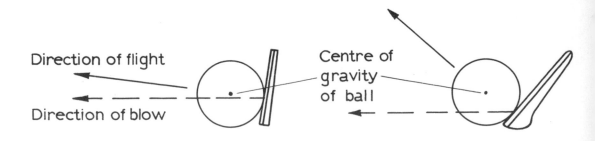

Direction of flight

Direction of blow

Centre of gravity of ball

are ahead of the ball at impact and the swing out-to-in, this will give quite a fair effect in sideways spin (making the ball curve to the right in its flight). With a short iron, on the other hand, you are always connecting nearer the bottom of the ball, so that if the hands get too far ahead and the swing out-to-in, you will still get a large proportion of backspin, and only a small proportion of sidespin. Therefore two shots hit with the same degree of lateness with a driver and a 9-iron will produce completely different results.

What we need is a whole set of clubs, from driver to wedge, so designed that there should never be any need for consciously earlier or later hitting, or any other sort of wrist-action adjustment.

As I write this, in 1963, there are signs that club manufacturers are catching up with the idea of real finesse in design to suit modern trends. I have already seen a set of irons with the blades opening as the loft increases. The makers (Messrs. Spalding) describe them by saying that the blades 'fan'. Most makers, too, are now putting a bit more loft on drivers, and turning the face slightly in, to suit the trend. A man who really drives the ball forward, needs what is in effect a deep-faced brassie, slightly shut. With a more normal driver, I could stop him cutting his drives, but I should have to do something to his swing which could spoil the rest of his game. If I gave him, for instance, a correction to his swing which would straighten out his driving, I might easily make him less good as an iron player.

Michael Bonallack two years ago was a very good player who tended to cut his drives. I changed his driver, rather than his swing.

Now this is not as out-of-this-world as anyone to whom this is a new idea might think. During the 1957 Ryder Cup match at Lindrick, I went into my cousin Jack's shop one evening, and looked through all the American team's bags of clubs. Practically every man's driver was lofted and pulled, and they had nearly all put their short irons in the vice and opened the faces beyond the angle to which the manufacturers originally set them.

I noticed, too, that their short irons had flatter lies than standard. That is, the angle between shaft and sole was wider than most manufacturers make them. This has much the same effect as opening the face, of course. The flatter any particular club lies, the more open will be the face; the more upright it lies, the more the face will close. With the flatter lie, the blade tends to open that much more on the backswing, and again this proved to me that the Americans guarded against hooking their short irons. They want these shots to come into the green quietly and stop quickly.

It follows from this that – even in general and throughout your set – if your tendency is to cut, you need clubs with a more upright lie; and if your tendency is to hook, you need clubs with a more flat lie. I remember one man who came to me for a lesson whose whole game I was able to change simply by altering the lie of his short irons. He was hooking them with his normal correct swing, and as soon as I flattened the lie for him, he hit them straight one after another. That man was only hooking shots because his clubs were too upright in lie for him. He was a very tall man, and had actually had some clubs made more upright than standard, giving himself as a result a hook he had never for one moment foreseen.

There was another man with the same trouble to whom I simply said: 'Here, hit one or two with my 9-iron.' I handed it to him and, with no change of method whatsoever, he hit them straight without further ado. (In fact, he actually talked me into letting him go away with my irons. Luckily, I had a set on the way over which Gary Player had selected for me in America, with exactly this sort of consideration in mind.) It's always worth bearing in mind, anyway; if you tend to hook your irons, particularly your short irons, try clubs with a flatter lie; if you tend to cut your irons, particularly your long irons, try a more upright lie.

*(Above) You may find your shorter
irons have a more upright lie –
giving in effect a more closed face
at address. I explain in this chapter why I think manufacturers
should open the face slightly more
with each increase in loft. (Right)
The deep face of a driver helps us
to hit the ball squarely at the
bottom of the swing arc. The
shallow 4-wood helps you get in to
the back of the ball in a tight lie*

But – let me repeat the warning – the
majority of present-day sets can enable you to
do both. We haven't yet in general – again, in
my opinion – got sets of clubs which enable
you to use exactly the same swing throughout the set and hit the ball straight with every
club.

Therefore, in order to do so, we have to

make adjustments which only serve to complicate the shot. I hope that the Spalding 'fanned' set is a sign of things to come.

Mild Steel

What about other trends in club making?

Well, first I think that mild-steel heads on irons are going to come in increasingly. Unfortunately they don't hold chrome as well as stainless steel, and therefore after a certain amount of use, they don't look as good. But I have noticed that, for instance in playing out of wet rough, you have more control of your ball with a mild steel face than with a stainless one. In America, moreover, a lot of the fairways are thick with clover, with a lot of juice in it, so that it becomes almost essential to play with mild steel. (Certainly British teams playing in America on a course with clover fairways have been at a definite disadvantage.)

Weight

If anything most people are playing with clubs too heavy for them. This is apt to make them hit the ball too much with the body instead of the hands and arms. Their shafts, too, are often too stiff for them to get any feel into the club without having a lot of weight in the head: more than is really good for them. With a stiff shaft, to a player of average ability, you have to have a heavy head to give the club any feel at all. When you have a long driving competition, it isn't the player with the heaviest driver who wins; it is the one who generates greatest momentum into the clubhead. The longest hitting professionals have been known to borrow ladies' drivers for long driving competitions. I myself often have woods made up for my men members with the stronger of the ladies' shafts put in – but I take the band off because most men don't like to feel that they are playing with a ladies' club!

This all ties up, of course, with:

Swing-weight

In my opinion we still have a lot to learn in this country about swing-weight. Swing-weight is simply the 'feel' of the club: how 'light' or 'heavy' it will actually swing. You can have two superficially identical looking clubs, both weighing 14 oz., and both 43 in. long, but which swing entirely differently, depending on the shaft, the grip weight and thickness, and so on. One could swing very heavily, and the other very lightly. For instance, a 14 oz. driver with a thick grip and an X-shaft would swing very lightly, while one with a thin grip and a ladies' shaft would swing very heavily. With the first one, more of the weight would be in the grip and the shaft, so that the head would be little felt. With the other, more of the weight would be in the head, at the end of the shaft, and it would thus be felt far too much.

One of the simplest ways variations in swing-weight can occur within one apparently identical set is in the simple matter of boring the head. Shafts are longer than they are needed and, tapering as they do, the exact boring of the head where it is to take the shaft is critical. If it is slightly over-bored then the shaft must be pushed that much further into the head before it fits tightly, and that much more of it in due course be cut off beyond the head; the more this is done, the stiffer the shaft will feel in play, since there will be more of the thicker part of the shaft in the club. If all the clubs in a set are not bored exactly to a most careful calculation of shaft setting, then variations of swing-weight can come into the set just like that.

It does sometimes seem to me that there is a variation of this kind between clubs in the same set.

Immediately after the war, when we could only get one shaft, I used to make myself a stiffer shaft, in effect, simply by boring out heads larger than standard, and pushing more of the shaft through to be cut off beyond the head, instead of at the grip end of the club.

Shape of Head

The main point here is that the old-fashioned type of elongated head is going to give you more toe action than does a shortened and compact head. The rest is very much a matter of personal feel and preference.

Depth of Face

Modern drivers tend to be deeper in the face than those of a previous era because we now realise we can drive the ball further if we hit it on the bottom, horizontal, part of the swing, which is difficult to do with a shallow-faced driver. Today we tee it high and hit it off the top of the tee, so that all the power being applied is forward and not downward, and we need the depth of face to do that. The shallow face is more designed for teeing the ball low and hitting it slightly down; a good way of driving straight, but not the best method for length. Similarly, when we are trying to pick a 4-wood out of a tight lie on the fairway, we need a shallower face in order to get more easily into the ball. Today, the difference between the four woods is not just a matter of loft, but equally of a progressive shallowing of the face, to help us get the ball out of tight lies. Sometimes the shallowing of the face so hides the look of the increasing loft that, to the eye, the woods seem to have much less difference in loft than you would find they had in fact if you measured them. This is an optical illusion; if one extends the face of a 4-wood to the depth of the driver the loft is very apparent.

Sand Irons and Wedges

Both these are absolutely essential. The sand-iron, with its round sliding sole, makes bunker play vastly easier than it is with a sharper-edged club; and the wedge correspondingly makes pitching much surer through the effect of its skid-sole. The wedge is very much in vogue today, not just because of this though, but because you can vary the height of the shot you want to play so easily; even when you hood the face, the skid-sole will still help you to get through the ball cleanly without chopping.

Putters

If you get the ball into the hole with it, then it is the right one for you!

Instruction: Where Are We Going?

A Standardised Method for Basic Factors

FIRST, I think the work of the Golf Foundation in teaching young players will have a profound effect. Some will take the game up, and become the best players. Others may not go straight on; but when they come back in their thirties and forties, they'll find the game much easier; and this is very important.

I think we'll get better teaching, more standardised from the beginning. It's when you are teaching a class of beginners that you most need a standardised method of instruction, a standardised system of what to tell them. This is where I think the P.G.A. are beginning to give a lead, although much remains to be done in the way of films, etc.

There's every reason for having a standardised method of teaching for beginners; but from then onwards, you really have to proceed with *methods*. Once you get beyond the basics of grip and stance and swing, you have to begin to take into account the peculiarities of each individual.

Let me make this quite clear. In any system of teaching there are these two aspects. First comes good sound practice. Then after that I

The Golf Foundation helps run golf instruction for classes of schoolchildren

think there's a much wider and much more general application: but something about which one can't lay too hard and fast rules, applying to every player.

Good practice, to begin with, includes teaching the orthodox way of swinging the

The P.G.A. are beginning to give a lead in the question of standardised instruction. Sid Scott is shown here with a class of young hopefuls

club back and through. This includes grip; stance and pivot; plane; and orthodox wrist action. I don't see any difficulties whatsoever in getting all professionals to agree on that.

Beginners are the only people to whom a method can be taught. It doesn't last long. Almost at once, people throw up and show up their own natural way of swinging. From then on they need individual attention.

From Universals to Individuals

Now we come to the argument side of the game: where some people say you should have a shut-bladed backswing, or a flat shoulder pivot, or an upright one. All those positions are correct, if they are balanced – this is where we come to methods. Only if a player's natural method is really bad, however, and not producing results, do you then have to

146

change it. More normally, you try to make him play as well as possible with the method natural to him. You will change and improve the method, *within* the method: not try to take him outside it.

One can see by a person's natural movements what method is suitable to him; you can also see the way he is thinking about it; and it all comes into how you decide to treat him.

Before you go very far with any beginner you will find he does have his method of playing. One person will open the blade more than the next person in the early part of the backswing, even though you have given them exactly the same basic instruction. This is as much mental as physical. Some people have an upright picture of the golf swing, and they are the shoulder-tilt people. Others have a rotary picture of the golf swing, and they are the flatter-turn people. You get soft-wristed and firm-wristed people too.

Now, I have the promising L.G.U. and E.G.U. pupils for instruction; in the beginning I have a heart-to-heart talk with them about the simplest way of playing the game of golf, and how to tell by the flight of the ball what their own natural tendencies are; but from then on it is individual instruction. I may spend only a few moments with one pupil, who has the hang of it, and then leave him or her for half an hour. With the next pupil I may spend a quarter of an hour before I can leave him or her for a while. The aim is to get them all playing *uncomplicated* golf – in their own natural way: natural and uncomplicated, so that it can be expected to work on the big occasion.

The 'Square' Idea

Misconceptions about the 'Square Method'

THE recent controversy, started and pursued by the magazine *Golf Monthly*, about the so-called 'square method' has had, on the whole, a good influence, if only because we in this country have for a long time over-emphasised wrist action and hand action. Certainly one cannot deny that it is the hands and wrists which generate speed in the club; everyone has come to realise this, and consequently underline it. But in my own opinion the best method to get speed into the hands and wrists is not to think about them doing this for you, any more than it is to rely on a particular body action to produce speed. It is all not primarily a matter of hand and wrist action, nor primarily a matter of body action, but a matter of being able to coordinate the two. We have talked and thought too much about wrist action. Telling pupils to 'use your hands' is, in my opinion, no guarantee that they are going to go ahead and use them correctly!

Now what 'square' ought to mean in golf terminology is this: *that the club-blade ought to be square to the way a person pivots.* To quote Bobby Jones on this: 'The position of the club-face is amply taken care of by the wind-up and unwind of the trunk.'

That, to my mind, is square-faced golf.

Someone who pivots with a flat shoulder-turn will have the club-blade more open at the half-way position than somebody who pivots with a more tilted shoulder action. At the half-way back position, their club-blades will be in different positions; but they can both be playing square-faced golf. In fact, when the club-blade is exactly in this relationship to the pivot, then you are playing square-faced golf;

The immortal Bobby Jones, shown above on his way to victory in the 1927 British Open, and left with the cup, had this to say about the 'square' method. 'The position of the club-face is amply taken care of by the wind-up and unwind of the trunk'

when it is not in this straightforward relationship to the pivot, then you are not playing square-faced golf.

In other words, we are trying to eliminate independent wrist action. But in trying to put that over, some people have *brought in* independent wrist action, through striving to – as they think – 'hold the blade square'.

Worse, many people seem to have got it into their heads that the more they keep the blade square to the intended line of play as they take the club back, the more they are play-

ing square-faced golf, when in fact, of course, they are only leading themselves into shut-faced golf. In order to take the club back as they are trying to, misguidedly thinking they are taking it back 'square', they are introducing a local and independent wrist movement, a turning of the wrists towards the ball as the club goes back from it, just as the opposite habit of rolling the club-face open involves turning the hands away from it. I repeat: the essence of what I should call square-faced golf is that there are *no* local or independent movements whatsoever.

The club-face can never stay square *to the ball*, in any case. It *must* gradually open to the ball on the backswing and gradually close again from the ball in the through-swing. The point is that this relationship is just and exactly that which naturally derives from the pivot and swing of the body, with the arms and club swinging accordingly in the plane set up by the body swing. No local and independent movement need be involved in this swinging away, and swinging back again, of the club-face.

The Value of the 'Square' Concept

Despite some of the misconceptions which have attended it, though, I do think that the prominence given to the idea of 'square' golf has been a good thing. Anything basically sound, however misunderstood by many, is likely to become properly understood in the end, and the more people begin to realise what 'square' golf does really involve, the better for many of them.

Another thing that is misunderstood from the 'square method' is that it does *not* dictate any particular club-face position at the top of the swing. This must always depend upon how much natural wrist action – within the momentum and plane of the swing – each player uses at that stage; and this, again of course, is determined largely by the amount of natural give in their wrists and hands.

I am, then, delighted with the 'square method' idea being brought to the fore (despite disagreeing with the way it has been put over on many occasions), especially in that it has killed the bogy of opening the blade *consciously* in the backswing and squaring it up again *consciously* in the striking of the ball. I don't think one can ever do that and still have all one's concentration on hitting the ball. The blade of the club should *feel* to be square throughout, and the hands should only cock during the backswing simply in order to enable them to deliver as big a blow at the ball as possible.

There *are* people, many of them, employing local independent wrist action, and still coming back as square to the ball at impact as they should have been at the address. But this is where the 'pressure' aspect of it comes in; under pressure, it *is* a bit more difficult to do, let alone to do consistently and reliably.

Utility Golf

Make the Stroke by Setting-up for it

THE manufacturing of special strokes for special problems, 'utility golf' as I call it, can be most necessary on occasions. But it is always noticeable that the finest players use the minimum amount of utility golf! If you bring 'feel' into ordinary golf, you are bringing in an unnecessary variable. It is obviously immensely important in the short game. But in the straightforward hitting of any *full* shot, it should be at its minimum, and then it is method which is absolutely important.

If you do *not* want a straightforward straight shot, you *set up whatever specific type of shot you want at address.*

The way you set yourself up for the shot will itself determine how you hit it. The method remains the same, but reacts to the variations in set-up for the stroke. You actually *make* the stroke at the address, and leave the rest to method!

For shots of varying height, using precisely the same method, no local independent variations are needed. For a high shot, you put the ball forward and drop the right shoulder so that you therefore pivot more underneath it. For a low shot, put it back and lift the right shoulder.

If you want to cut the ball, you open your stance and put the ball forward. This will set the body across the ball. You now pivot and swing to that stance; and you would obviously take a grip which makes sure that the blade is open. The hands, however, will be in sympathy with the body action and with the target, and therefore will resist any rollover at impact, anyway.

If you want to hook a ball, you close your stance and bring the ball back a little, which is going to make your swing in-to-out; you take a slightly hooky grip, and as you pivot through the shot, your hands will this time want to help the club through to the target. In this case, you'd hurry the hand action and slow down the hips; the opposite of the cut, when you'd hurry the hip action and delay the hand action.

There still needn't be any *independent* opening or closing of the club-face at all. You can just train a consistent method to react of its own accord to *variations in setting up* for whatever sort of stroke you want. I think that is really the key to consistency, even in utility golf.

Last Resort Last

Independent wrist action still remains, of course, as a last resort; and it is fair to say that utility golf in its extremer forms does call for more conscious use of the hands than any other sort. The average golfer should certainly, for his own benefit, be taught to hook and slice. I always teach my assistants how to hit these shots, first by setting up the stance for them, and only then by consciously using the hands as well.

The change of hand action, I repeat though, is still much more achieved by the set of the stance and therefore the pivot. The hands get in sympathy and will do what you want them to do the more readily. I am all for simplifying method, even in utility golf. When you are playing under pressure, you want to eliminate as much pure 'feel' as possible.

What We Can Learn from the Americans

(i) *New Simplicity in Young Players*

IT is already noticeable that amongst the younger members of the American Walker Cup and Curtis Cup teams, there is much more similarity than there used to be; the reason being, of course, that they have all been reared on much the same golfing lines. The first real time that fact seemed to run through a whole team was in the Curtis Cup match at Lindrick, when the young ladies all seemed to be playing very much the same simple game; this was underlined by the wide variations in method and swing of our own team, who played near their best, but were beaten very convincingly. Simplicity. Turn, swing; that's all those American girls did; then turn through, and let it fly.

In America during the last decade I do think they have been standardising the simple way of playing golf; and since, by their age, that Curtis Cup team had all learned during this period, they were the first to show this uniformity. I think that what has happened in America will happen over here to some degree.

The young American Walker Cup players

Deane Beman (right), Richard Sikes (below) and Labron Harris (over the page), all members of the 1963 American Walker Cup team, show the similarity which comes from being reared on the same golfing lines

are showing clear signs of the trend, too, though this is somewhat cloaked, up to now, by the high average age of American amateur teams.

How soon we catch up with this new trend ahead of us in American golf is anybody's guess; but it need not be long. In fact it can be just as soon as we realise that the swing is based on a sound grip, stance and pivot, *and cut out anything which is unnecessary*. Our young players must be taught like this right from the start.

(ii) *Youth is not everything*

However important it is, though, to look ahead to the young players for any future talent of international calibre, it seems to me at the same time that we have had too much accent on youth in international selection. I've nothing but respect for the people at present in charge of amateur selection. Their enthusiasm is most genuine; they give a lot of time and money to the task, and they think hard. But I do think the one mistake they have made is to push some youngsters ahead too fast.

A young fellow of 18 may have a great deal of potential, but if he is not really as good or reliable as a man of 40, I'd pick the man of 40 every time. Potential is not everything in golf. It has got to be realised in achievement, and backed with experience. I myself teach a number of amateur golfers in their thirties and forties whom I would be prepared to back against some of the youngsters in international teams. Nor is the ease with which the young learn in general all that matters. There are players of around 35 who come to me with a swing very near the simple ideal, and some of them I can help in a very short time. Their immediate potential, with the experience they already have – had they time – is possibly greater than some of the bright youngsters'!

My feeling is that the typical promising youngster needs to be very well taught in the soundest possible way, but that it is not a scrap of good pushing him into international competition until he is really ready for it; and certainly not before he is as good as the person he is going to displace from a team. Youth is not everything, nor is a man old in golf at 40 – as the American Walker Cup selectors so amply demonstrated in their 1961 side, which included Bill Hyndman, Frank Taylor and Bob Cochran; all nearer 50 than 40. The captain of Wales, Albert Evans, won his native championship again in his fiftieth year, and led his side admirably in the 1961 internationals (though I must admit that

American Walker Cup player Labron Harris

eight of the other Welshmen were in their twenties when they beat England for the first time in 1961). There are many people for whom the game of golf does not end when they reach 40, or even 50. Rees and Snead, to name only two most obvious examples, are getting very close to the half-century.

What matters is not just for someone to be a good player on his day, but to be a *sound* player. What we want to do is to teach our most promising young players the simplest possible method which will help them to become good *and* sound players – in the longer run; so that when they eventually do come to play in international golf, they will be able just to play their normal game.

(iii) *Method and the Walker Cup*

We are always going to be up against it, of course, when playing America. It's not just the argument of numbers, though that is bound to be telling. It is also that a number of their leading amateurs make a tremendous amount of money, not exactly *out* of the game but around and about it. They are neither cheating nor infringing their amateur status, but inevitably they meet a lot of people and get introductions thrown at them. And when, for instance, you are selling insurance, or practising a profession in some special field, then you may get on much more quickly and easily than a man who has not the same scope in meeting people.

The American Walker Cup players tend to have a lot more freedom to play the game, and more incentive to practise. To be at the front over there is to be worth meeting; and to be worth meeting opens a lot of doors! Some of them have the opportunity to practise their games about ten times more than someone like me is able to over here! Most of our Walker Cup players, on the other hand, have to work hard for their living; and always will have to.

Much has been made in the past about the British team's tendency to lose the first two or three and the last two or three holes, on balance, to the Americans in Walker Cup matches. I've never thought that this is any matter of courage, self-control or guts. It is just the strictest comparison between methods under pressure. It's a fact, that, in comparison with the typical American-type, compact method, our own amateur swings have just too many screws loose!

When it counts most, the looseness tells; and certainly in Walker Cup golf to lose more than one of the first four holes goes a long way towards losing the match – let alone the second real pressure-patch at the end of the match. In Walker Cup matches I have watched, the Americans kept a tighter relationship between body and club-head, and this seemed to be the really decisive difference accounting for the determining

breaks over those first and last holes. As a matter of fact, I think much the same goes for the Ryder Cup matches – if my fellow professionals will forgive me for saying so. With them, as with the amateurs, it is not a matter of any disparity of courage or 'being quick off the mark' or 'staying power'; it is basically a matter of reliability of method of the very highest order, when the nervous tension is at its highest.

I don't really think that the series of American victories can be ascribed either to any superiority in their pitching, chipping and putting. It may have been true some years back, but it doesn't seem to me true today. I do think, though, that in the short game, and particularly putting at that level, you have got to be decisive, and that the American move away from a swinging stroke towards a tapping or rapping one has contributed to the all-round tightness of their games.

Looking ahead in general over the whole field of golf, I venture to make one prediction which sums up in outward appearance all I have been saying. I think from now on the best players will begin to look more and more alike as swingers, since the co-ordination of body and wrist action will become substantially the same; and the determining mark of success. Of course, everybody will never look like everyone else, but the basic similarity will be there, and amongst top players simplicity will show itself more and more in dominance.

This will not mean that the picture will ever be dull and uniform. No two human beings are the same, and different bodies and temperaments will express basically similar mechanics in different ways. The endless variety and contrast of personalities and temperaments will be all the more fascinating, for the more generally uniform reliability of method.

Looking at the Simple Swing— and Seeing it Several Ways

(i) *Synchronising Body and Hands*

ANOTHER way of underlining what I've been trying to say might be worth adding here. It is one more simple view of the swing, which can help a lot of people to get a better grip on the essence of playing golf simply. Put it like this:

Golf is not played exclusively with the hands; nor is it played exclusively with the body. The whole art of the game is to synchronise body action with hand and wrist action. You just can't play well enough with either alone. From this angle, we can put the general thesis even more simply: *Wind-up and swing; then unwind and swing*. The wind-up and unwind takes care of the blade of the club, leaving the hands and arms free to hit.

If your body action stops at any stage, you will then get independent hand and wrist action. You've simply got to keep swinging both your arms and club and your body. You want a sort of continuous motion with the body and arms, letting the hands do the hitting.

You must let the swing generate its own centrifugal force, like a child on a swing. Turn and swing; turn and swing. If you get the relationship right, you feel your body has to move – you can't swing the club if it doesn't.

(ii) *Where the Swing begins*

Here's another way of looking at the golf swing.

You play golf from the inside, rather than the outside: you start the swing from the hub of the wheel rather than the spoke.

The hub will throw its momentum in a particular direction, and the wheel will follow. The spokes are not rigid; the arms and club link the hub and the rim of the wheel, and that linkage will look after itself. You can look on the action between the arms and the shaft as one connected via a universal joint in the hands and wrists. This does not mean that the joint is a sloppy one! On the contrary, you want to make it a firm one, to preserve the connection between hub and rim. But – depending on you – it is a joint which *can* allow movement in any direction, and this means simply that the direction will tend automatically to follow the impulse given to it by the direction and momentum of the swing of the hub.

The hub – the pivot and body swing, that is – decides on what path the club-head is to travel, and the hands and arms let it follow that path, and then do their hitting within that path.

(iii) *Hips and Hitting*

Of course we all have our own ideas about the way golf is most likely to develop. And as far as method goes, I foresee a new era when we finally throw off the yoke of complicated swinging, and just work on a sound grip and stance, pivot with a straight left arm and pivot back with a straight right arm. It all boils down to a simple picture of what you are trying to do. If you can keep it simple, and then keep your hips going through the ball fast enough, you can hit just as hard as you *can* keep your hips going through the ball.

This may be a helpful way of putting it, again, to some people. Let's expand, then.

If you want to hit a quiet shot, then the

shoulders turn in the backswing and the hips turn in the through-swing *slowly*, and the hands and arms synchronise to that. But if you want to hit a ball hard, you have to hit it with your legs and hips much faster. This is where most players fall into trouble, unless they realise how important this part of your body is to the shot. You can only hit as hard as your leg action and hip action are up to.

In the old days we were taught to sling the club from the top; but the real point is that only as long as you are winding and unwinding properly can you sling as hard as you like.

(iv) *Aim and Let Fly*

I think most good players ought to feel that they aim the shot (in other words they stand correctly); then they should simply feel that they turn their back on the target. In doing that, through the momentum of the club-head, the wrists will cock. Then they get the hips cracking towards the target, and hit at the same time.

The over-all feeling is of turning your back on the target and then facing it, and giving the ball a good hit while you're doing it. This cuts out any conscious worry about the blade. Do

Address, top of the backswing and impact positions of the simple swing which I discuss in this chapter

remember that any trying to hold the blade square in the backswing is just as conscious an effort as trying to roll it open. The feeling should simply be one of holding the club with your hands. Turn, and let the hands work in whatever plane of turn you have chosen.

This is not quite the same thing as the 'one piece' idea. You can turn *and* you can break – but in the right relationship.

(v) *Live or Dead Hands?*

Over the last few years, there's been a lot of argument about the relative merits of 'live' and 'dead' hands. This is really nothing to do with the general problem of the golf swing at all. The issue is an artificial one, artificially widened. I think that the 'live' hands people have been those who think in terms of independent conscious hand-action; but calling those of us who do not believe in *independent conscious* hand-action 'dead' hands people is quite incorrect. I have even been called the 'dead hands merchant', which couldn't be further from the truth, even though the whole theme of this is against having any hand and arm action independent from the body movement.

(vi) *Club-head and Body*

Another way of casting some light on the troubles of many of us is by looking at our general method in the light of the relationship between body and club-head – as a direct entity. With us the screws are too loose! There should be a very direct relationship between the club-head and the body. If you are going to hit hard, then you can only hit hard on the basis of keeping that relationship firm.

It is amazing how you can keep a tremendous amount of club-head speed without softening your wrist action at all. One knows a lot of people who hit the ball a long way without any sort of sloppiness of wrist-cock. I suspect that the amount of wrist-cock does not, in fact, have a great amount of bearing on how far you can hit the modern golf ball. If you can hit the ball a mile without any wrist-cock, as some can, then why bother with any at all?

The general answer, and key to the whole question of how much wrist-cock to have, is I think simply this: you need just as much wrist-cock as is dictated by the suppleness of your wrists and hands. If the grip is firm and the direct connection is maintained between body and hands, then the wrist-cock will be almost automatically dictated by the natural give in your wrists.

Wrist-cock should proceed from your swing and the nature of your wrists themselves – not be superimposed consciously upon it. It should be dependent on the swing, not independently added to it.

(vii) *Make Golf Simple*

The most successful swings in the world today are not as classic as those of earlier eras – the most beautiful of all of which was probably that of Bobby Jones. But the essence of them is the same. The difference is dictated by the differences in clubs and balls. The torsionless steel shaft and the highly lively ball make the long flowing swing no longer necessary. You can get exactly the same result nowadays, as the Bobby Jones type swing used to give, despite chopping off two feet of the backswing. The backswing is only needed to get the forward- and through-swing going: and with today's equipment you don't need so much of it to hit the ball consistently well.

This fact itself helps consistency, because it is any delicate stretched parts of the swing which fail under pressure; the more compact and firm you can make the swing, the less there is to go wrong. The best players today are all uncomplicated. Perhaps Dai Rees, still

Of all the players who formed their swings in earlier years, Dai Rees has probably the simplest of them all

at his best in his fiftieth year, makes – within the general context of swings formed in earlier years – the simplest example of all.

We must remember, at the same time, that the average age of golf professionals in the British Isles is still high enough for by far the majority of us to have learned our own golf in an era that required the fuller swing. We still have the feeling, in the back of our minds, that the glorious way of playing golf is more attractive than the solidly simple business-like way.

The Americans, on the other hand, have never had such a long tradition to unlearn as we have. They come straight at it with a fresh approach, and streamline all the best of other people's experience. No doubt the Russians will, in due course, do the same thing – and that will be when international competition will get really tough!

(viii) *Getting There*

In the sections of this chapter above I have, as the reader will have noticed, repeated myself a number of times. But I have done so in different terms each time.

There is a simple reason for this. We do not all react to words in the same way, and the differences in our imagination, particularly about a thing so subjective as golf, makes different people more likely to grasp an idea in different ways. Put it one way and maybe forty in a hundred will get it; put it another way and another twenty will get it, and so on.

I have hoped that by putting the essence of what I am saying in a series of overlapping statements (or pictures if you like) looked at from different angles, I have helped to give the basic concept of the simple, easy, un-complicated golf swing, form, shape and content for the reader.

Pure Golf

THERE are two distinct parts to this book: the Analytical – which it is useful to understand when you come to putting faults right – and what I call 'Pure Golf', which is how I think a club can best be swung.

The Analytical is to put things right, to get these golf swings neutral, so that I can go on to tell them about 'Pure Golf', which is simple golf.

The second aim, then, was to make golf simple; explain the golf swing in terms of its easiest essentials.

I began the book by doing this at some length and in some detail; and here I'd like to try to sum it up in its greatest simplicity. Let's put it in a series of short, intentionally overlapping statements.

1. You need a good grip and a good stance.
2. The grip will determine whether the club-blade is square to the line of aim when you hit the ball, while your arms and hands are left free to do the hitting.
3. The right stance is essential if you are going to be able to pivot and swing the club correctly back from the ball. So turn the shoulders, swing the arms and cock the wrists, all in plane to the top of the back-swing.
4. I started the book by explaining the concept of the 'swinging wrist-cock'. I'm now trying to put it even more simply. From the hips downwards you maintain your address position, and stay 'sat down'; the hips will still be *dragged* round to some extent by the turn of the shoulders, but they will stay in a 'ready' position for starting the downswing.
5. Now, how does this go on? It all ties up together and balances, backswing to through-swing. Let's now just unwind the hips, swing the arms down at the same time and uncock the wrists through the ball.
6. In other words: wind up the shoulders, swing the arms and cock the wrists; then unwind the hips, swing the arms down and uncock the wrists.
7. Carry on the unwind of the hips, the swing of the arms and the uncocking of the wrists through impact up into the follow-through.

This to me is the essence of the golf swing. You can call it the square method or any method you like. But I just call it the simplest way of playing golf. This method is the easiest, and the best method must really be the simplest and easiest one.

All teaching, to me, should aim simply to knock out the superfluous extras on top of the simple basic swing.

What I've Tried To Do in this Book

Tracing Symptoms back to Causes

I'D like to make one thing clear about the aim I have had in writing this book. It is certainly not guaranteed to bring you down to scratch. It is not, in fact, *guaranteed* to bring you down at all.

My aim is to help people to play better golf

by first understanding the mechanics of the swing, so that they can help themselves to do away with everything unnecessary in developing a complete and powerful action, which can readily be made repetitive. The reader has to turn my words into feelings.

My belief is that no book in the world can ever be a substitute for a lesson from a qualified professional. However hard we try, and however intelligently we try, none of us can be certain of diagnosing our own faults correctly. We may be able to see and feel what is going wrong, but almost always it takes someone else, and someone highly

right basically, but also – *and I am sure this is tremendously important* – exactly how and why that basic error leads to the surface errors, the symptoms, which we are ourselves aware of.

Now the more the player knows about golf, and the more interested he is in the mechanics of it, the easier becomes the instructor's task in making this explanation to him, and the more readily will the player cotton on to it, and be able to employ it in putting his game right, from the essential corrections given to him. If he really understands the why and how of golf, then as soon as his instructor points out where the trouble is beginning, he

qualified to do so, to diagnose where the trouble *is beginning*. We may ourselves be quite right about the symptoms. But the fundamental cause may appear only to someone outside. Between the two there will be a chain of causation. The instructor's job will then not just be to tell us what needs to be put

may even be able to see the rest himself, without further explanation. (This, of course, is how it usually is with professionals when we diagnose each others' troubles during tournaments.)

Here we have the aim of the book. Not to put your game right automatically (though, of course, I hope it will help many people on its own); but to help the reader to understand how golf's various errors begin and tie up with each other. It is aimed as a contribution to the reader's general understanding of the game, and to set out clearly the tools of analysis the professional will use to help him.

I have covered, or tried to cover, every important aspect of the golf swing. There's a tremendous amount of information about it in the book. Obviously you can't think of all this information when you are trying to play golf. It may be only one little thing which is fundamentally wrong with your game, which you can't find out for yourself, nor yourself arrive at by tracing it back from the various surface symptoms which you are all too familiar with. The good instructor can tell immediately what is wrong, and give you simple corrections to think about while you are playing and practising. All the rest of the analytical part of this book will then, I hope, help you to understand *why* that is what you have to think about.

Let me give an example. Many people are aware they are 'hitting the ball too much with the right shoulder', for instance, but comparatively few of them realise that they are getting into a position at the top of the back-swing which makes it a certainty that they will 'hit with the right shoulder'. It is what is wrong *there* that the instructor will diagnose for them.

Once accept that a good instructor is the only real answer for anyone wishing to improve, then we can agree wholeheartedly that reading a golf book is a good way of learning golf. Anyone who plays the game for pleasure will get a lot of pleasure from reading about it too; so let's all enjoy ourselves and read.

I hope, then, that this book, read intelligently, may lead people I'll never see to ask the right questions about themselves, for one thing; and to think intelligently about the golf swing as it relates to their own method, so that when they are in trouble, then the explanation will ring a bell with them from what they have read and studied. The man who has really taken in the practical mechanics of golf from a book does, in fact, when it comes to taking instruction, hugely help the professional to help him.